MOTHER TRUCKER

An Urban Couple Downshifts to Life on the Road

Shelley Hamel with David O. Hamel

For David

ACKNOWLEDGEMENT

As much as anyone's, the words in this book are David's. If you read anything funny, David probably wrote it. If you read anything uncommonly smart, mechanical or technical, David wrote it. Credit me with stringing the story along, in my voice, but as the experience was a collaboration so is the authorship whether borrowed from journals or letters home. Thanks to you, David, for some wild rides.

INTRODUCTION

I 've whined my whole life that I do nothing well. In my dreams, I'd like to be a concert pianist. But scratch that — I can't hum the first note of "Happy Birthday." It's doubtful piano would come easily.

So, the time came to face facts and find another way to earn a living. This book is about how my husband, David, and I earned ours. We crewed on a charter sailboat, patented an invention, worked for nice bosses and bad bosses, and drove a semi (aka 18-wheeler, big rig) for three years. Most of our married life, we worked together and enjoyed it, except for the times we hated it. If there is a theme to this book, it's to team up with someone who recognizes the door to adventure and, if necessary, pushes you through its keyhole.

NOTE TO READER

Many things have changed in the truck driving universe since this book was first written, especially "hours of service." If you are thinking of making truck driving your career, be sure you are aware of all current Department of Transportation regulations. *Westfield WI, 2017*

4

1

I'm driving, David's in the sleeper berth. Interstate 84 east of Scranton is torn up for major reconstruction. It's been that way for two years and today, in pouring rain, I'm bullying a little old lady in a red 4-wheeler by crowding her right fender, slicing the edge off my side of the white line that separates us so she'll slow down just enough to let me in the left lane. A half mile ago, an orange construction zone sign warned, "MERGING TRAFFIC – ALL TRAFFIC USE LEFT LANE.' I'm a big truck. I'm in the right lane. I'm seventy-five feet long, weigh 80,000 pounds, my left turn signal has been flashing for half a mile and now my trailer tandems are nudging her over because if she doesn't wake up and let me out of this goddamn right lane, in an eighth of a mile I'll be wedged into concrete barriers separating us from construction company dump trucks. I can see her face in the West Coast mirror between the high-octane swipes of her wipers. She's hunched up over the steering wheel, locked in a death grip, terrified. Her passenger, a teenager, is giving me the finger up tight against his windshield. I'm tempted to return the gesture but instead I back off the throttle, switch on the 4-ways and begin my own mini traffic jam, slowing down to wait for a courteous left lane driver to create my escape hatch. Another semi driver interrupts chatter on the CB, "Schneider, c'mon over! Your lane ends. I'll let you in here." I see a pale yellow J.B. Hunt semi two cars behind the little old lady, so I downshift, matching my speed to the gap created by J.B., still mildly pissed at the stupid driver in the red car whose lack of highway courtesy or common sense almost forced me to a dead stop on the interstate. As I drift back past the red car, that kid still has his happy finger in the window. I shoot back a peace sign 'V' and give him a good look at my smiling face so he'll know he's being obscene with a middle-aged woman his mother's age, and the finger disappears.

David always lets me drive this stretch of highway. Threading in and out of narrow work lanes, through construction zones, weaving through traffic around Scranton is woman's work. It's the only part of truck driving I do well. I've maneuvered through this construction zone enough times you'd think I wouldn't be in the right lane, but the problem is, every time – even if our trips through here are just a day apart – the configuration will change, new concrete berms, different work zones, different weather, but always one lane bumper to bumper traffic.

J.B. Hunt dips his headlights to signal me in, "C'mon Schneider, you're clear". Until I answered, "Thanks J.B." he didn't know he was dealing with a woman driver, a "beaver" in dirty truck lingo. So he gets all friendly and talkative, which wakes up David. CB talking is one of my least favorite things. David knows this, climbs from the sleeper berth into the passenger seat, takes the mic, and has a short but nice talk with JB about weather.

I never quite understood the mechanics of how to drive the big truck – even though I did it for three years – so I wouldn't be your best teacher if this book were a learner's manual. David's the one who ought to write that book. He caught on to double-clutching right away. Mechanical engineer, and besides, boys have this in their genes. They're borne double-clutching. All those kicks in the womb: that's your boy child double-clutching. I'd never heard of double-clutching until driving school up in Green Bay. Furthermore, it took me the whole first year to figure out basic ten-speed shifting so I could do it smooth enough and not wake David up while he was trying to sleep back there in the bunk. Jerked him awake every time. Stall. Re-start the big ol' diesel. Wopawopawapa. And lurch away.

I'm pretty sure he never slept through my shifting. He'd shout out of his dream, "Sixth gear, lower left, sixth gear, you missed it, fifth gear, fifth gear, upper right, switch down!" The only time he slept uninterrupted was when we'd switch drivers at an interstate rest stop in Nebraska or Nevada, one of the wider states, and I'd roll down the highway for hundreds of miles, unless the weigh scales were open, and then I'd have to pull in, get weighed, and lurch out. David couldn't sleep through that even though at weigh scales I tried extra hard to drive smoothly because I had an audience sitting there in the scale house and one in suspended animation in the bunk. I sweated through those scales.

Once in Colorado, the scale master actually came out of the scale house, climbed up the side of my truck, and scolded me for not understanding that the red light meant "pull on to the scales" and didn't mean "stop" like every other red light in every other state of the Union means. Just not in Colorado. Not only did I get scolded, he did a whole Department of Transportation safety check on the truck which delayed us an hour. So forever after, when we approached a Colorado scale house, I'd make David drive through. Even if he was sleeping, I'd pull off on an exit ramp, wake him up and make him drive. He was surprisingly good-natured about it. (Real truckers call scale houses "chicken coops" or plain old "coops," as in "Them coops open over your shoulder?".)

I believed, deep in my heart, there was a prejudice against women drivers in Colorado. Because once by accident, I forgot to pull off, change drivers, and make

David drive the big truck through the scales. So there I was, driving, and again, that damn guy at mile marker seventeen got me. Even though I understood the lights that time and miraculously rolled onto the scales like grease on a skillet. He looked me in the eyes from his glass cage. David's convinced the guy just had a crush on me. His nasty voice crackled in the intercom by my open truck window: "Pull ahead and park. Bring in your papers." He wanted to see everything, so I had to park, find the bills of lading, check to make sure my log book was in order, make sure David's was in order, and get into the scale house before the guy suspected I was fudging the logbooks. Which I would never do anyway, because I strictly obey the law. But not necessarily convention.

Ever since meeting David in 1978 and marrying him two years later, we've periodically breached the boundaries of convention and wandered outside what our friends and families consider a middle-class work ethic. Some envy us; others resent it. We suspect that's because — except for personal encumbrances —they'd also be doing something unconventional, maybe even foolhardy.

I'll divert here briefly because this part of our work history sets the stage for what kinds of risks we were willing to take to stay out of the office – any office. Our first breach came in 1979 when we ran away to Annapolis, shortly after finding ourselves suddenly single, leaving our kids (three of his and two of mine) with our ex's for eight months, abandoning our jobs, family and friends to embark on our first work adventure. We had mailed out about ten query letters to all sorts of sailing charter companies just to see what kind of crew opportunities existed out there. Most had written back telling us to just "come on down" to Tortola or the Virgin Islands, hang around the marinas, read the bulletin boards, and maybe, just maybe, we'd get lucky and find a crew position. That struck us as an expensive way to read a bulletin board. And this was well before the internet. So imagine our exaltation when one company, Stevens Yachts of Annapolis, offered us jobs as part of a delivery crew from Annapolis to St.

Lucia in the Windward Islands. They'd give us airfare back and a possible job once we arrived. Breathless, we accepted. Next, we ran to the world atlas to find St. Lucia.

At the end of three energetic weeks, we had our Madison house rented, our eighty-pound dog farmed out to a helpful but unwitting neighbor, our Chevy van packed, and final paychecks from our employers deposited in skimpy bank accounts. My final act was to get a haircut and low maintenance perm, something I wish I'd given more consideration. I left town that October looking like Bozo.

We never really expected to be offered the skipper and first mate positions when we got to the West Indies since, except for the trip from Annapolis, our sailing qualifications were limited to Saturday races on Lake Monona in our second-hand 20-foot C-scow sailboat. David could read nautical charts, having spent every summer since he was a teenager on Rainy Lake in Ontario, Canada, at his family's island cabin. Other than being able to fix anything mechanical on a boat, his open ocean sailing qualifications had been nil. But we had made a point of emphasizing what skills we did have (I could cook) in our query letter to Stevens Yachts and demonstrating our best can-do attitudes to Trevor Robertson, the thirty-year old delivery skipper, on our seventeen-day trip to St. Lucia. Nobody, at least up to that point, had called our obvious bluff even though Trevor spotted us diving into the cabin to look up some cryptic nautical terms when he asked David to "seize and mouse the anchor shackle."

Either the ruse worked or Ian Cohen, the St. Lucia manager, was out of options because he shook hands, said "Hello, that's your boat out on the mooring. Move your stuff there because you can't sleep on St. Lucia without a work permit. *Running Free's* first charter arrives Sunday." Maybe Ian was implementing an affirmative action policy – we were the first Americans of the two dozen or so crews in the Stevens Yachts St. Lucia fleet operation. We were, by far, the oldest. The deal was we lived on the boat all the time, got paid $400 a month for David and $175 for me, and whenever there was a charter for *Running Free*, we were the crew. When we weren't on charter, we anchored in Rodney Bay, a small dredged lagoon so polluted that at night, you could see fish streaking through a wake of bioluminescence.

But I'm ahead of myself. First there was the little matter of learning to sail *Running Free*, a 47' Gulf Star motorsailer. We had to learn about anchorages, clearing customs, snorkeling locations, navigating. For four days, an experienced crew from South Africa gave us a crash course up and down as many islands and anchorages we could fit in before our first paying charter, honeymooners from California, climbed over the transom scuppers.

Fifteen years later, we'd find ourselves in the same position not only learning to operate another kind of over-sized vehicle but struggling again with a career-changing mind-set. It's clear we were never comfortable with the concept of "careers." You can't run away if what you want most is to march along a career path toward a pot of gold and a 401-K. But we'd never had a penny in a retirement plan, and if you think about it, had we had a penny, the decision would have been exponentially more difficult. Our doctor friends, lawyer friends, executive friends were mid-way through successful careers forged after years of consistent goodwill, alliances, longevity, and pension planning. David had grown up in Madison where some of his high school buddies were its pillars.

When we decided to drive a truck, our kids were all fledged. Even so, we broke the conventional wisdom of our middle-class, white-collar worker friends who had little experience and even less envy for a stereotyped life of blue collar work. They knew we didn't know what we were getting ourselves into. But David seldom meets a physical or conceptual challenge he doesn't think he's up to. I'm not like that at all. I'm a doubter. Except in the case of truck driving: that was my bright idea, and I had no doubt this was to be the adventure of a lifetime.

We turned ordinary truck driving into the best of all road trips. Sailing had been our first lesson working at the system fringes, to make our own luck by forging ahead with an unconventional idea one leap at a time. Although we leapt without much planning and little experience, we were fortunate to have the resources and energy to learn quickly, act reliably, and have a blast. It had been a lark; it had been a risk. It had been worth it.

And my mother, were she living, would have approved no part of it.

2

In the fifteen years between sailing and truck driving, we had several other "real" jobs. Each in turn would reaffirm our determination to get out of the office. David, using his engineering meal ticket, found consulting jobs. The only thing that kept them from being too boring was to buy a used motorcycle to drive the three miles back and forth from home to office. While he was there, no amount of machine design made him satisfied.

One of the things I did was become a department head at a start-up toy company in Madison called Pleasant Company, later sold to Mattel for a bazillion dollars and renamed The American Girls. I was just the second hire at that wildly successful company, and before I left, as Director of Product Development, I'd learned almost everything there was to know about making toys in China. But, what a misnomer – *Pleasant* Company. Life in that company wasn't pleasant, and I was still operating under the principle that work is supposed to be fun. David often says that there's usually a pretty good reason why "work" is called "work." Sailing had been the exception.

And if we hadn't faced personal bankruptcy, our best real job during the period was manufacturing a patented invention of David's called the "Starplate Building System" for geodesic backyard buildings. With an ambitious and talented partner, we started from scratch, made money hand over fist for three years, only to be knocked off by a larger, richer company, forced into an expensive patent lawsuit and ultimately bought out by our enemies, the company that knocked us off. Our partner, Ulrich Sielaff, less disillusioned with entrepreneurial adventure than we, went on to become the sole proprietor of a furniture design and manufacturing company. Today, he's fabulously successful. Luckily, we all got out of that little Starplate business with a roof over our heads and because we are by nature frugal, even had a few pennies left.

During periods of weekly paychecks from real jobs, our payoff was stability and regular contributions to savings. Yet for the next decade and a half, we'd trade those benefits for a course of mixed unpredictability, invention, risk, responsibility and adventure. We needed to pay the mortgage, but more importantly we needed to stay curious about life.

And we had learned on the boat when we were never more than 47' apart that, except for anchoring, we enjoyed working together, so we aimed to do more of that some day. During our learning curve on the boat, the daily two-man process of anchoring in wind and current strained our ability and patience. But over the years we conveniently forgot about our near mutinies during those anchoring experiences. Were it not for the presence of high-paying charterers witnessing our every word, we would have damned each other from bow to stern and back again. Like the pain of childbirth, such memories of working and fighting in close quarters fade.

Finally, in 1995, David was designing machinery in a small family-run business where he was not family. It was on an "as-needed" basis, but it was a paycheck, nothing more. I'd left Pleasant Company and was intermittently consulting in the toy business with periodic trips to China with David accompanying me. His time-study skills led to a year's employment in Hong Kong for a toy business associate of ours, and he became far more accustomed to the intricacies of travel there and in China than I did.

Slow periods as consultants were normal and expected. Neither of us was old enough nor rich enough to retire, yet we were too old to launch new careers, too lazy to hustle, and too bored and uninspired to think like the Starplate entrepreneurs we once were. We had no job security, a sketchy future, and we were being forced to make big changes. It was probably the best thing that ever happened to us.

The situation came to a head around Memorial Day when, after a week's vacation, the son in the family-run business called David in for a one-day job. His desk and computer had been moved elsewhere, so he did the job on a spare computer, working out of a cardboard box full of his reference materials that had been cleaned out of his desk. All this desk moving was caused by "sales department growth" and, the son said, would soon settle down. David was asked to take his box of stuff home and wait for the phone to ring. It never did.

Now for the first time ever, David was showing up in the unemployment line. I thought it was humiliating, but it didn't seem to bother him. He'd been on the paying in side for thirty years; he felt it was his turn to take a little out. As part of Wisconsin unemployment obligations, he was applying for jobs almost everywhere in the Midwest. In years of experience, he was worth three times what anyone was offering, not that they were offering. Nobody, it seemed, wanted a fifty-seven-year-old with his plucky, rebellious ponytail, and David was becoming intractable about settling for just any old office job.

Friends, having seen glimmers of success with our China connections, urged us to expand it, to find new customers who needed go-fers to travel halfway around the world, finding factories and troubleshooting international commerce nightmares. It was compelling, but it wasn't happening. Besides, it was a gamble every time we went to China that we'd survive the latest flu mutation flourishing in the soupy fish ponds of Guangzhou province. Twice, after that long trans-Pacific airline trip, David had taken me directly from the airport to the hospital with new and unusual sinus infections. What was next – cholera, hepatitis, meningitis, dengue fever?

Having lived in the back of my mind for many years, the idea of being a truck driver was quietly working its way toward the front. It worked its way past the crummy bosses I'd known, past office politics, subterfuge, even foreign travel and was emerging as the single greatest idea I'd ever had. It didn't matter that I didn't have a clue about what trucking was really like. I could imagine.

Ads for over-the-road (OTR) drivers were everywhere, column inch after column inch. This was the single greatest idea emerging again. I had visions of the open road, the truck radio blaring golden oldies from the 50's, 60's, and 70's and serenading us down highways I'd traveled as a kid, endless hours of books-on-tape, and my smart, mechanically-inclined husband at the wheel, a guy who could back up boat trailers in his sleep. It seemed almost patriotic for us to move the nation's commerce. A professional driver. I'd never had a bona fide profession in my life. It was about time!

I can't quite remember David's initial reaction to this upwelling of enthusiasm, but it wasn't "Hell no, never!" If he doubted anything, it was a trucker's income. Even that was not for long. I pulled out the classifieds and showed him the ads. Team drivers – two persons sharing the cab and driving round the clock – could earn $45,000 in 1996 dollars per year – each!

The "team" concept was something we latched onto right away. We enjoyed being involved in each other's workday, and we enjoyed each other's company. We reviewed our situation. As self-employed people for the previous decade, we'd paid our own annual health insurance premiums of $3000 (in 1995 dollars) with annual deductibles of $2500 each. As relatively healthy adults in our mid-fifties, these deductibles were never met, so premiums and office visits were out-of-pocket. We'd never had company-paid retirement plans. We'd never had stock options. We'd only dreamed of paid vacations. Our friends had all these things, but at what price? They were office prisoners.

The notion of landing a job that paid both of us to work together, away from the big office environment, to travel, to be our own bosses with very little stress or financial risk seemed like asking for the moon, when that still had meaning. Sure, we could clerk at the same store or flip burgers at the same joint, but things were not yet that desperate.

As we thought about it, the worst things about other jobs didn't seem to apply to truck driving. Truckers were free as birds, out on their own, touring the country doing straightforward work. How hard could it be to sit back, switch on cruise control and tick off the miles?

It was time to find out whether trucking could roll us comfortably into retirement. We drove ourselves up to the Sun Prairie Diesel Driving School just north of Madison one cloudy afternoon to talk to a real driver. Fluorescent cones snaked around an obstacle course. Big red and white trucks with the words "Student Driver" stenciled on in foot-high letters on the trailer were parked neatly along one edge of the asphalt lot. Was that to keep the students humble, or was it to give the rest of the world fair warning?

An enthusiastic salesman named Wayne met us at the school office, lit up a cigarette, and escorted us to an empty classroom. Our questions spilled out, mine first:

How hard *is* it to drive a big truck? Can a fifty-year-old weakling like me do it? How long does it take to learn? What's it like to be on the road?

Wayne was sharply insightful. He could tell how nervous I was about maneuvering that huge truck. "Can you drive a shift car?" he asked.

I gestured out the window to our Dodge Colt Vista with 104,000 original miles. "Five forward gears," I said. "Plus reverse."

"You can drive a truck," he declared. I believed him with all my heart.

Then David's questions: Is it better to be an owner/operator or drive a company truck? How much money could we make? What's tuition at the Sun Prairie Driving School? Was Wayne ever a driver?

Wayne had been a driver. He said he loved being on the road. He handed us a diesel driving school brochure, told us tuition was $3700 each for three weeks of training. After graduation, which meant passing the state-administered commercial drivers test, the school promised to help find us a job. He showed us long lists of trucking companies and contacts posted to the bulletin board in the hall. Many looked like the same names from the newspaper. Finding a job would be the least of our worries. As we departed, Wayne took me aside and pointed reassuringly to the most recent graduation class photo. One woman stood in the second row among twenty-two male classmates.

The idea began to grow on David. Next morning, he was dialing the "800" number of a dozen different trucking companies. Most were looking for drivers with a year or more of experience. Some, however, would train totally inexperienced people like us for a $1,500 to $2,000 fee that is forgiven after a year of loyalty to the company. J.B. Hunt in Little Rock had a four-week school which cost $2,000 each. H.O. Wolding in southern Wisconsin required a $1,600 training fee. And many companies were willing to recruit inexperienced recent graduates of a driver training school like the one in Sun

Prairie. Covenant Transport in Chattanooga kept rookie graduates with a trainer driver for four months before they could team together.

David created a computer spreadsheet with a row for each company. He assigned variables to weighted columns, variables like cost of schooling, length of schooling, expected income for the first three months, pay rate after three months, age and type of tractors, time at home, nearest company terminal, benefits. But in the end it all boiled down to how we were going to get trained. After that we'd be qualified to go anywhere.

Next, he talked to a few vocational schools. They were cheap enough, but at one or two days a week, the training took four to six months, longer than we wanted to spend. Then he discovered that right in our own backyard, just a booming punt away from Green Bay's Lambeau field, Schneider National Incorporated, the largest truckload hauler in the world, has its headquarters and its own truck driving school. How much was tuition at Schneider? Nothing, and it included free room and board! How long would it take? Two weeks! Two weeks to learn to drive a big truck.

Not only that, when the recruiter on the phone found out we wanted to be a team, his enthusiasm spiked. Teams, he explained, move freight farther faster because they can split driving duties while staying within strictly regulated allowable driving hours. Schneider loved teams. The deal they offered was free school, a free ride to school, free meals while in school, free lodging in Green Bay and after graduation, you get to drive one of their bright orange "pumpkin" trucks. No contract, no obligations. His main question to us, "When can you start?" Schneider sorted to the top of the spreadsheet.

That afternoon, David drove to the two semi-tractor sales offices on the outskirts of Madison, climbed into the cabs of Peterbilts and Kenworths, gathered dozens of color pamphlets, and reported back. After looking at the wide-angle shots of cushy cab interiors, I was dying to climb into one, too. So we drove back to the Peterbilt dealer together and climbed up (way up) into their latest and greatest tractor.

It was metallic ruby red. It was a conventional cab (also called a "hood") configured with the engine way up front under a hood and a miniature bedroom behind the drivers' seats. There was a little floor space back there, closets, and a pair of twin size bunks; one at normal seated height, one above.

"Cab-overs," as their name implies, have the sleeping and driving cab directly over the engine. The only floor space in a cab-over is in front of each seat. There's a flat engine cover about elbow height between the seats and immediately behind the seats is one big bunk, also about shoulder height. You have to crawl from the seat back into the bunk on your hands and knees. You can't stand up to get dressed; it's like dressing in a pup tent. Cab-over wheelbases are much shorter than conventionals, and we were assured that the cab-over ride was much rougher. Today, they've been replaced for the most part by conventionals.

The sticker price for the ruby-red conventional tractor was about $90,000 in 1995 dollars. When you add a microwave and television, a laptop and refrigerator, stereo speakers in the sleeper bunk, and custom paint job, the price escalated to well over $120,000 but that included chrome lugs on the six wheel covers and extra twinkle lights everywhere.

Of course, our image of life in a semi truck was pure fantasy. The only conversation we'd ever had with a living-breathing trucker was during a project a few years earlier when we had a dozen containers of used car tires loaded and shipped to Hong Kong, bound for China. During one loading at a tire salvage yard in Minnesota we marveled at the way a stunning young blond truck driver wiggled her trailer into a very cramped makeshift loading dock. It hadn't looked possible. Talking to her while her trailer was ricked with rows of tires, she told us she took up driving because her boy friend was a dirt hauler on construction projects. Normally they worked in tandem, he in his truck and she in hers. We asked what the hardest part about truck driving was. She gave it two seconds' thought: "Stupid men."

What else could we learn about this strange, new kind of life? Across the road from the dealer, we pulled into a truck stop and took seats, a little self-consciously, at the restaurant's "Drivers only" section. We looked around for couples like ourselves, soul mates ditching corporate America, choosing adventure over ambition. We found one. Most of the drivers were chain-smoking, overweight solo men. But we did eavesdrop on one couple having dinner and finally, I got enough courage to ask the woman, who was a tiny little thing, what it was like to drive a big truck.

"Well," she said in a smoker's voice, "these new trucks are simple. We've been driving ten years, and every year the trucks get more comfortable, easier to shift, or I'm getting taller, or both. And power steering is just like in your car."

Her husband, in his smoker's voice, chimed in. "I used to do all the parking, but now she's better than I am."

These two were owner-operators, driving their own truck, signed on to a big trucking company. They asked who we were planning to drive for, and we mentioned Schneider. We started talking about how many cents a mile they were paid ($0.82/mile), and then they explained how being owner-operators meant they paid their own fuel, insurance and maintenance costs plus monthly payments to payoff their $100,000 tractor. Since one of our goals was to simplify our lives, owning our own truck was a step in the wrong direction.

They were headed upstairs to do their laundry, so we tagged along past another "Drivers Only" sign to see what upstairs looked like. We peeked into a spacious shower room that was being cleaned. It was spotless. There was even a telephone on the wall and a hair dryer next to the sink. A few drivers were in the smoking lounge watching television, a couple of them having fallen fast asleep, and a row of telephone booths lined one side, half of them occupied with drivers.

One of our new friends said, "Schneider has a good reputation for getting loads. See those guys on the phone? They're talking to a dispatcher somewhere, trying to find a load out of here so they don't have to deadhead. That eats up your time, eats up your pay. It can ruin your life." They wished us good luck, and we thanked them for our first peek into the driver's inner sanctum.

Next morning David called Schneider and scheduled an interview for the two of us at their Milwaukee operating center for the end of June. There was no doubt they'd be happy to get an applicant like David, a fit 58-year old mechanical engineer who'd quit college just long enough to join the Air Force and fly single engine, all-weather jet interceptors. During his office days, he had been very preppy and conservative but now he sported a full beard and pony tail, looking more off-beat than a grandfather should. From what we'd seen under feathered cowboy hats at the truck stop, that wouldn't disqualify him.

But then there was the second half of the team. I had little natural mechanical aptitude and had spent most of my life working in offices. Other than a perfect driving record, my only qualification was being able to drive a manual transmission car. Reality was beginning to worm its way past my naive excitement. This, for me, was to be a big stretch. Would the interviewer size me up, see through my enthusiasm and find any real qualifications to handle an 80,000 pound vehicle? No slam dunk, this.

Dennis, a former driver-turned-recruiter wearing a black-and-orange company shirt, met us in the clean and tasteful lobby of Schneider's offices just off I-94 south of the city. He was an amiable thirty-year-old. He handed us each a thick booklet and lead pencil, pointed to separate rooms, and told us to take the 45-minute test.

It was a strange test, mostly a psychological questionnaire looking for clues about latent recklessness with questions about sky diving and Indy car racing. I was a non-risk-taker so if a question asked whether I ever had ambitions to be a sky-diver or rock-climber, I answered "no." On the other side of the wall, ex-fighter-pilot David was answering "yes."

Dennis pulled out a tall stack of forms to fill out our work histories. We reviewed the training program, pay schedule, holiday/vacation policy, medical insurance. We signed off on the pushing, pulling and lifting requirements. We watched a video about life on the road alerting married solo driver candidates to changes their domestic life would take. It was a good pilot for a daytime soap opera. We handed over our driver's licenses so they could do an immediate records check. After all this paperwork, we figured we'd be excused, and they'd let us know in a week or two whether we could take step two.

But after disappearing for fifteen minutes Dennis reemerged, stuck out his right hand, presented us with black-and-orange ballpoint pens and welcomed us with a hearty handshake into the Schneider family. It was the quickest, easiest job offer we'd ever received. As he pushed back from the table and prepared to say goodbye, he offered one piece of advice. "David," he said, "Schneider drivers are company representatives and must be clean, neat and well-groomed. You might want to have your hair and beard cut." It was the first and last time anyone mentioned that crazy idea.

It was almost lunchtime, and we were almost Schneider employees so we sauntered into the employee's cafeteria. The room was half full of drivers chowing down. Loading up our plates, we fit right in and joined two drivers at their table. First thing we wanted to know was their CB handle. We'd learn later that such handles are obsolete, but one driver called himself the "Eveready Bunny" because, he grinned, he keeps "going, and going, and going." The Eveready Bunny told us a good war story about getting stuck in gridlock in Manhattan where he had to make a turn at an intersection and an illegally parked car was making it impossible. A New York cop stepped up on his running board and told him to clear out, and if he had to run over the illegal parker, so be it. Eveready Bunny put it in low and dragged his trailer tandems right up and over the hood of the car. You're never sure how to respond to a story like that.

On our way home with bellies full of truck stop food, we felt a strange, new kinship beginning to develop with the semis we passed. We celebrated our giant step in a new direction by splitting the apple pie á la mode at a Madison truck stop.

The time had come to break the exciting news to our family and friends. Up to now, no one had a clue we were considering such a radical move. Among our regular circle there are typical academic types, white-collar administrators, artists, teachers, lawyers, doctors, and politicians. Running away from home to go sailing brought out envy; this could bring out something else.

Not too many nights later when about ten of our friends assembled for our regular Sunday movie group and potluck, we mentioned that we'd been thinking of becoming over-the-road truck drivers and had, indeed, been offered jobs by the largest trucking company in the world. We had black-and-orange ballpoint pens to prove it. They were incredulous.

"You'll wreck your kidneys! You'll ruin your heath! Interstates are awful! It's winter, wait 'till spring! It's dangerous! You'll hate it! You've gotta be kidding! You'll break your back!" they blathered.

We countered, "We'll find a way to exercise. New truck seats are designed to oscillate so they're easy on backs and gentle to kidneys. Interstates can be beautiful. Gotta learn winter driving sooner or later, might as well be sooner. See America first! Offices suck!"

Our white-collar, well-meaning, middle-aged friends thought we were crazy. Some were even a little accusatory, like we were abdicating responsibility. But David's three grown children and both of mine were surprisingly comfortable with the news. Although they never said anything, David always thought his kids would have preferred being able to introduce friends to their-father-the-Bank-President or something. Over the phone, of course, it's hard to tell, but my son who was worrying his way through graduate school at Princeton, and my daughter who was apprenticing as a boat builder in Maine, seemed at peace with the idea of their mother, the trucker.

3

S uddenly, things were moving apace. David and I troubled over the logistics of it all, although keeping with the traditional division of duties, I troubled more. Thank god the dog and cat were dead and the kids grown. But: should we sell our house to cut expenses? What would our neighbors say if we parked an orange semi in front of our house? Could we legally park a semi in front of our house in this upscale, waterfront neighborhood? Would it hit the telephone wires over the driveway? How would we get from the semi to our house if we couldn't park the semi in front of it? Can you just park a semi at any old truck stop and leave it there for a weekend? How do you get home from the truck stop? What truck stop? Maybe we should keep the house and rent it out in case we were failures at truck driving? Was all this talk premature? Could I really learn to back the damn thing up? I couldn't back a boat trailer. What made me think I could back a semi? Who would water the plants?

I remembered that years ago I was determined to learn to sail a boat, too. I enrolled in dinghy sailing lessons at the University of Wisconsin one summer, and before ever getting into a boat, I read everything I could about sailing. But the little wind direction arrows near the tiny boat illustrations didn't correlate with tiller placement and sail location in my mind, and the prospect of tipping over or ramming the dock in front of the lunch time crowd at the Student Union terrified me. So, in preparation, I'd retire to the bedroom and sail my bed through the windows of the bedroom, back in through the door, dock at the closet, tack into the hall and jibe back out, and visualize the whole sailing gestalt, wind arrows and all. I could do the same thing with a semi.

But first, the written test. The Schneider offer was contingent on first passing this state-administered commercial drivers license (CDL) written test. With learner's permit in hand, Schneider would teach us how to pass the CDL driving test at their Green Bay location and follow it with two weeks of over-the-road, on-the-job experience with individual trainers. After that, David and I would rejoin and be assigned our own truck from the pumpkin patch.

Next day, we stopped by the Department of Transportation to pick up a copy of the Wisconsin Commercial Driver's Manual, nearly seventy pages of written rules, tips, and instructions for driving every type of commercial vehicle. Schneider required drivers to have the hazardous materials (hazmat) endorsement. I shuffled the pages back to the hazmat section. A paragraph began, "A driver transporting chlorine in cargo tanks must have an approved gas mask in the vehicle. The driver must also have an emergency kit for controlling leaks in dome cover plate fittings on the cargo tank." Holy shit, I thought. Is hauling hazardous materials really what rookie drivers should be doing?

Besides hazmat, we'd be tested on the pre-trip vehicle inspection (pre-trip) which covers twenty physical areas of your basic truck and includes one-hundred thirty-four safety checkpoints. Next: turning, stopping, parking, driving safety, air brakes, spring breaks, parking brakes, air tanks, coupling, uncoupling, and emergencies. We could skip getting endorsements to drive tankers or doubles/triples (sometimes called "double-bottoms" and "wiggle wagons") which are those trucks with extra trailers and look like a short highway freight train.

I read the fine print in the manual to see if there were any aids I could use to remember the classes and chemical descriptions of hazardous materials. Not any. Chemistry never was my strong suit. David said the manual looked much easier than the Hong Kong Pleasure Craft Master's study guide. He added that passing the Air Force entrance exam was certainly much harder. This was not helpful information.

On the day of the test, it was like being a nervous sixteen-year-old all over again as we drove up to the Division of Motor Vehicles Service Center. I figured that with a little luck, I could be as intuitive as the twelve men in line with me would be. No doubt we'd all get the one right about whether or not it was proper procedure to transport poison gas in the driver's cab.

The test booklet was thick. Sections about bus driving and chauffeuring were omitted because these were "endorsements" we wouldn't need. Also omitted were test sections for doubles/triples and tank endorsements which I had decided to forego. If Schneider wanted a doubles/triples driver, it wasn't going to be me. David could probably do it, but I wasn't interested in driving something that long going that fast.

David finished in forty-five minutes. It took me an hour. I couldn't remember the maximum number of feet a truck carrying hazardous material had to stop before a railroad track. I forgot the part about carrying an emergency kit to fix the leak in the chlorine tank. I was confused about the supply line and the emergency line to the trailer. I didn't know how many psi (pounds per square inch) were lost when the engine was turned off and the brakes applied or how many minutes it should take. But I thought I knew most everything else. I also knew I'd forget it all as soon as I walked out of the building.

The official behind the counter graded the test while I watched. I think I missed about eight, maybe ten. He threw away the answer sheet and asked for twenty dollars. This was the first hint I'd passed.

David was waiting in the car, napping. Driving home, reflective, I savored this little triumph – the test respectably passed (David missed just one), two CDL learner's permits in hand, ready to roll. At home in the mailbox was a video tape from Schneider, the same one we'd seen in Milwaukee during our recruitment. We popped it in and watched the first ten minutes again, the part about new "driver-husbands" being away for weeks at a stretch, and eager little children running out to greet their dads after miserably long absences and wives trying to repair cars on their own. Wives became single mothers overnight. For people with families, truck driving seemed to suck.

I imagined us in a much more amiable situation. I imagined us listening to endless hours of books-on-tape, visiting new parts of the country like Biloxi, surveying the country for out-of-the-way retirement homesteads tucked into little dead-end canyons, downloading *The New York Times* from a cellular phone connection to our new laptop, never really being out of touch, but being totally out of reach.

I imagined us driving hard for a week in our big orange truck, pulling up to our destination in Pocatello, Idaho, for instance and stopping there long enough to rent a car for a day's worth of bird watching in the nearby foothills. David and I are avid birdwatchers. I didn't know for sure if there even were foothills in Pocatello, but that's just the kind of adventure I imagined us having – finding out the truth about Pocatello.

Then came the part in the video about Green Bay training. There was a mind-bending scene of Schneider's famous "skid pad," a euphemism for the insanely slippery (and in the winter – icy) asphalt parking lot where students accompanied by their instructors deliberately go into uncontrolled skids in a flat-bed semi, steering madly to get out of it. It was NASCAR on ice. Backing up a semi suddenly seemed no problem compared to the skid pad.

Now, I love a good adventure. I'm in front on a toboggan. I detour to ride roller coasters at theme parks. When I was thirty-eight, I was easily coaxed into an Italian acrobatic plane. We did barrel-rolls and a hammerhead stall or two. Neither made me sick. On the lake in front of our house, David and I spent some blustery days whipping around in an ancient iceboat we inherited, clattering across expansion cracks on Lake Monona. But, as I said, sky-diving and rock-climbing were not part of my scene. Neither were skid pads. I began to worry.

There was one last follow-up interview with the Schneider rep before we reported to Green Bay in the middle of February. One last chance for us to back out before beginning. One last look around for something compelling that would keep us off the skid pad.

Coincidentally, the Wisconsin Motor Carrier Association was having their annual trade show at the Dane County Exposition Center, so to warm up for the interview we immersed ourselves in trucking stuff for an hour. Dozens of information booths set up by manufacturers and service organizations jammed the building. But the excitement for us was long rows of gleaming, sparkling tractors on display with stand-up sleepers and luxury custom interiors.

Here under one roof were Kenworth, White, Freightliner, Mack, Volvo, Ford, Peterbilt and Western Star tractors. We climbed into one after the other to get the feel of what life would be like. Some were cramped, some roomy, depending on how many comforts-of-home the customizer squeezed in. Some felt like hearses, others like a rock star's tour bus. Our favorite had a daybed that converted to a cushy sofa – perfect for company to join us for a beer and watch the Packer game on a 14-inch television mounted to an upholstered sidewall and flanked by state-of-the-art speakers. David tested the clutch on that Freightliner and got a little discouraged. For a couple of years, his left knee had had a kink, and he wasn't sure it would hold up under stop and go traffic conditions riding a stiff clutch for an hour. If it was stiff for him, how about for my girly knee?

Our biggest concern with Schneider at the time was their exclusive use of short, cramped cab-over tractors. Were we starting down the road of least comfort and convenience with Schneider's obsolete equipment? From a beginner's point of view, the good thing about a cab-over is that you have a bird's-eye view of the front fenders. They're right under your nose, so it's supposed to be easy to keep them out of trouble in tight spots. Besides, we'd heard that to attract experienced drivers, Schneider was finally switching to conventional tractors. That was great news.

David picked up more literature. Roehl Transport, another Wisconsin company, handed out a brochure titled *"Ten questions you should ask about the trucking companies trying to hire you."* This was getting complicated. Our goal was a simple life of driving, eating and sleeping. Instead, in a dozen different brochures came the complex business of comparing pay policies with every permutation of: incentive pay for miles, down time, seniority, pick-ups, drops, loading, unloading, tarping, layovers, detention time, bobtail miles, empty miles, fuel efficiency, percent of time overspeed, on-time delivery, safety, training, annual miles, New York City deliveries, Canada border crossings, vacation and profit sharing. This was way beyond David's early spreadsheet. We were lazy. Schneider was the default choice, the quickest way to get started, and if it turned out their equipment was miserable, we'd just take our CDL's across the state and join up with someone else.

So we stopped shopping around and got over to the last Schneider interview being held at the Hampton Motel. John, the interviewer, needed to update our original driver training school applications. He brought us back to earth the minute we sat down. First thing he pushed across the table was the brand new two-part form, "Covenant not to Compete." Trainees were now being asked to pay back the $2500 training cost if they took a job with some other trucking company within a year of being hired by Schneider. They'd finally caught on that they were being used as a training school for all the other companies. It seemed fair enough, so we signed it.

Then he cut to the chase and asked David, "So, exactly what have you driven?"

David replied, "Well, I started with bikes, lawn mowers, and outboard motor boats. Moved up to sail boats, cars, farm tractors, a potato chip van, twenty-foot Winnebago, four different military jet fighters and two prop jobs, some ocean-going sailing yachts, and a sixty-foot twin diesel motor yacht on the South China Sea."

"Ever drive a semi?"

"No, you've got me there."

But we passed the interview, again, with no comments about David's ponytail or beard this time. Before we finished, John picked up the phone and called Schneider headquarters to ask whether teams from Madison were needed to run something he called the "Kimberly Highway."

After he hung up, he asked, "How would you like to run the Kimberly-Clark dedicated runs from Appleton, Wisconsin to Ogden Utah, Los Angeles, Paris Texas, and South Carolina? Living in Madison, we could get you home regularly. It's all drop and hook, easy runs, lots of business, and you'd earn big mileage."

"What's drop and hook?" I asked.

"You drop one trailer and hook up to another. No unloading. No loading. Easy. Predictable. You learn the route, you learn the yards, you'll love it."

He made it sound so special, so we agreed to start with the Kimberly Highway. At least until it got boring. In fact, I was relieved there would be less chance of getting lost in strange cities while we climbed the learning curve.

There were just a few details left at this point. We needed a state-required medical exam which John scheduled at a local walk-in clinic. We gave him several personal references to contact to make sure we hadn't embezzled money or murdered anyone. But mostly, I was thinking about a to-do list as if there were no tomorrow. For example, even though it was February I worried about who would mow the lawn in May, who would weed the garden in June, July, August, and September. I worried about whether it made sense to have a security system installed since we'd never be home, have a post office box or pay a kid to collect the mail, cancel one of the two phone lines, sell one of the two cars, stop insurance on the car we weren't using, sell the house itself. With a list like this, we weren't simplifying anything.

We started ticking things off by going to the walk-in clinic. I'd never been to a walk-in clinic before and never had a drug test before, but Schneider was paying for this state-required medical exam and routine drug screening, so we went where they told us. Pasted to the wall by the bathroom door were instructions regarding the big test. The rules said that when a male was being tested, the technician could accompany him into the bathroom and stand in the adjacent stall. Oh great. I looked for the part about females. Nothing. Then the technician asked me to take off my coat, take everything from my pockets, leave my purse on a hook, and with a stern look, warned me not to flush the toilet or wash my hands until instructed. I went inside, and he stood right outside the door at his lab station. More instructions were posted over the toilet. They warned that water was controlled from outside the room, and we should not tamper with the on-off valves under the sink. The thought hadn't occurred to me although, obviously, it does to some.

I came out and handed him the sample. He took one look and told me I'd failed – not enough urine in the cup. So I chugalugged six more cups of refrigerated water and waited for it to percolate. When at last I handed the cup back to the technician, he gave permission to wash my hands and flush the toilet. He asked me to witness while he poured the urine into a vial which had a clever built-in thermometer, sealed it in front of me, put it into a special pouch, and then asked me to sign a multi-part chain of custody form as well as initial serial-numbered adhesive seals on the package. I wondered how you could cheat even if you wanted to.

Next, I was shuffled into an examining room where Dr. Goodman, the walk-in clinic doctor who had just finished seeing a worker's compensation patient with a broken leg, asked skeptically, "So you're going to be a truck driver?" He didn't wait for an answer. "Well, you know what you're going to hate about it?" He answered the question himself. "The boredom. These drivers, and I don't mean to be disparaging," he said disparagingly, "with IQ's between 80 and 100 have to concentrate their entire brains on just getting that 18-wheeler down the road. I see a lot of them. Believe me, you are going to hate it."

This was another one of those times when you just don't know what to say.

David's turn came. While he'd been waiting, he'd filled out his medical history questionnaire. A long list of ailments was preceded by the words, "Do you currently, have you recently, or have you ever had (fill in the blank)." That word "ever" covers a lot of history. He admitted to a stuffy nose, headache, back pain, surgery (appendix), asthma, blood disease (mononucleosis), cramps, nausea, loose stool, lost consciousness, dizziness, shortness of breath, coughing spells. He admitted to almost everything.

But he didn't admit to the ruptured disc in 1983. That was during our Starplate days when we were importing carriage bolts from Taiwan, and he'd spent two days single-handedly unloading truckloads with a pallet jack. To budge the heavy pallets, he'd wedge between them, sit on the floor, and push with his legs. The next day he sneezed – just one sneeze – which knocked him to the floor, unable to move. Ulrich and I carried him downstairs, loaded him into the van and took him to the hospital with a typical ruptured L5/S1 lumbar disc. He spent the next few days in traction.

Chiropractors, acupuncture, hospital back school, self-help tapes, exercises, and special cushions did little but keep him slightly crippled for the next couple of years. Over time his back healed, and like millions of other Americans, he considered a little pain once in a while normal. So he answered "yes" to the back pain question but forgot to mention the hospitalization, intending to deal with the examiner's questions when they came.

There were other self-incriminating true/false questions like, "Have you experienced periods of forgetfulness?" Another asked, "Have you ever experienced difficulty making decisions?" He left the answer blank and wrote in the margin, "Can't decide." When Dr. Goodman saw that answer, he didn't chuckle.

There was another tense moment when the doctor pulled a rubber glove onto his right hand and asked David to drop his pants so he could check his prostate gland. At a different clinic a month earlier, he'd had the same test and been given a clean bill of health. David tried to fast talk the nice doctor out of doing another finger probe. Once every few years was too much, but twice a month was cruel. After a couple of coughs to check for hernia, the glove came off, the pants came up, and David couldn't believe his good luck.

The subject of back pain never came up. So we got our brand new CDL medical certificates and were headed for Green Bay. After that, whenever anyone asked what it took to become a truck driver, David would always reply, "When you exhale, does your breath fog a mirror?

4

I'd been through a variety of schools. I'd been through elementary school, high school, through college, even through graduate school. I'd taken refresher courses in this and that. I took life drawing at a vocational school. I'd studied real estate on my own, passed the state exam. I wasn't a particularly stellar student in any of those schools except maybe elementary school when I got rave reviews in sixth grade because of the nearly life-size peacock I drew feather by feather. David had even been to flight school. But neither of us had been to trucking school.

It was February 16 when we pulled into the Excel Inn in Green Bay, all our gear packed for two weeks of motel living. Before we left Madison, the last domestic chore was to water twenty-two African violets lined up on the kitchen windowsill, the spindly Norfolk Island pine dying in the living room, the split leaf philodendron, the two blooming geraniums in the upstairs bedrooms. But when it came time to water the budding amaryllis, my heart stopped. I'd nurtured this amaryllis for six years, a

Christmas gift from David's sister. Last year it hadn't bloomed. I'd followed instructions and put it in a dark place for six weeks. This year it had the biggest bud of its life at the top of an eighteen-inch stalk. No way was it staying behind.

Actually, not much stayed behind. Green Bay, like the rest of Wisconsin, is famous for its winters. No unprepared person ought to be outside for long bitter days learning about truck parts in the middle of February in northern Wisconsin. So we prepared like Boy Scouts. David brought two winter coats. I brought two winter coats. David had at least two pairs of boots and one pair of shoes. I had the same. David had a ski hat, and I took a full face mask, three wool hats, one six-foot hand-knit scarf, two knitted neck warmers, two pairs of lined gloves, one pair of buckskin work gloves, one pair of glove liners. We each had long underwear, two pairs. I had four sweaters, four pairs of slacks. But the jewel in my wardrobe was a brand new pair of Wall's "Blizzard-pruf" insulated working guy bib overalls. And David had his. David had his special pillow. I had mine.

We boxed up a kitchen's worth of breakfast. Instant oatmeal, grapefruits, oranges, yogurt, UV milk that doesn't need refrigeration, a jar of sugar, cookies, bran muffins, Rice Krispies, Bran Buds (David refuses to eat Bran Buds but they were left over from making the bran muffins), dried prunes, dried apricots. Plus, just in case we needed a snack during the evening's television, some cheese and sausage, rice cakes, crackers, and cookies. In the cooler, we had Coke and beer.

We packed the laptop computer and used its carrying case for a portable office complete with pre-addressed envelopes, stamps, the Madison telephone book, a small stapler, yellow highlighters, rulers. We each had flashlights stowed somewhere deep in one of the four duffel bags.

The receptionist at the Excel Inn didn't notice how much we were moving into room 107. She was too busy checking in the lobby full of other Schneider students, all male. No one seemed to notice the eighteen-inch amaryllis go sneaking by.

It was clear from that moment – the moment in the lobby – that this was not to be a smoke-free environment. The poor old Excel Inn, clean as it was, friendly as it was, suffers through hundreds of smoking trucking students a month. By the time we made it down the hall to our room, our life expectancies had been slashed by a decade.

We unpacked, stuffing both dresser drawers, lining the perimeter of the room with various boots, foodstuffs, empty duffels, partially full duffels, food bags, coolers. David's hair potions and my two tiny cosmetic bags, his ditty bag, my hair dryer, his toothbrush and toothpaste, my toothbrush and toothpaste and 50.7 ounce bottle of Cool Mint Listerine cluttered the bathroom counter. The amaryllis sat on top of the television.

We were not light-packers. How the hell would we fit into the cab of a semi? I chewed on that as I drifted off, alarm set for 5:30 AM, a tiny bit apprehensive about tomorrow's trucking school. Not so much because it was "back to school" again after thirty-five years, but if the lobby was any indication, this was a man's world. Roughneck guys with rough language in rough clothes handling big trucks, all chain-smoking.

Our fellow students were assembled in the lobby the next morning by 7 AM. I scanned the crowd looking for females. Saw one, then a second scattered among forty or so men, many standing outside smoking on a bright, cold morning. David spotted a familiar Madison face, Joe Heggestad, an old high school acquaintance and westside Madison fixture. He owned the Regent Street Market, a tiny neighborhood grocery in an area where many University of Wisconsin professors and their families live. Everyone loved Joe and gave him a huge party when he retired at age fifty-five. A year later he was bored. Why was *he* here?

His story, similar to many we'd be hearing in the coming weeks, was that the best parts of the grocery business were the stories truck drivers told him while unloading his merchandise at the dock every week. The worst part was the confinement of working sixteen-hour days in the one-room store, then going upstairs to his apartment to eat overripe fruit from the produce section. Retirement bored him, so here he was, ready to see the world. We couldn't believe it. Neither could he.

When our names were called, we stuffed ourselves into the specially-equipped laundry room at the Excel Inn. Alongside a row of washing machines were three very special chairs outfitted with 9-speed Fuller gearshift mock-ups. This was my first hands-on exposure to the gearshift, and more importantly, to the gearshift handle. It was as big as a baseball, too big to really grip. And it had a lever – a small half-inch plastic flip switch, sticking out three inches down along the far side, too hard to reach with girly fingers. This was not my Dodge Colt Vista.

A black-and-orange Schneider representative squeezed into the room, reviewed the schedule for the upcoming week and explained – prematurely I thought – the check-out procedure. We were told to completely empty our rooms of all personal possessions, and leave our room doors propped open, or we wouldn't graduate. I think they were worried about TV sets.

The overcrowded briefing out of the way, we boarded two Schneider-orange school buses on a cold, clear morning and headed over to the Schneider Training Center, about a five minute ride from the motel. Our bus driver, a regular Schneider trainer who was to be our classroom instructor, displayed what we would come to recognize as a professional driver trademark: his head moved constantly, glancing from mirror to mirror, swiveling side to side, never stopping for more than a few seconds. He spent as much time looking behind him in the mirrors, alongside the length of the bus, as he did looking in front. We, too, soon would be bobble-heads.

We pulled up to the training center, a long, low building surrounded by parking lots of orange trucks, some hooked up to trailers, some not. The ones not hooked up are called "bobtails," an affectionate term, I thought. Anthropomorphic. Cuddly.

Inside, we assembled in a double-sized carpeted classroom behind long tables arranged in a "U." We were invited to free coffee and free snacks in the capacious dining area on the other side of the hall, and while most of the class took this short opportunity to go smoke, the rest loaded up on donuts and scalding coffee. I took a closer look at my classmates. There were about seventy of us now, two busloads' full, and all but four of us were men with bellies.

The women looked younger, although one short blonde may have been my age. She'd weathered. Another hadn't been watching her weight. The third, in her late-twenties, was missing some critical teeth. Two of them acknowledged me with half-smiles.

When the last smoke was extinguished in the snow bank outside, class re-assembled and we were introduced to Wayne Lubner, a Schneider vice-president. Tall, clean-shaven, in a robust voice he explained that normally Don Schneider himself gives this welcome speech to new recruits but since Don was out of town, Wayne was substituting. He touched on the company's mission statement, then jumped right to the practicalities of being the nation's largest truckload hauler, how each driver or team managed a mini-business, responsible entirely for its profitability. Twelve thousand drivers times twelve thousand mini-businesses added up to a privately-held company with $1.75 billion annual sales back in 1996. Schneider, for most of us, would be the biggest company we'd ever worked for, by far.

To stay profitable back then, the company enforced a 55 mph speed limit even if the posted limit was higher. It was hugely unpopular, but Schneider saved fuel, lives and money by driving slower and, in fact, some drivers refused to drive for Schneider for what they believed was this wimpy policy. Speed kills. I secretly cheered the policy. It automatically screened out reckless cowboy drivers. A year later they changed it.

Further, Wayne warned that if our tachometer regularly climbed into the high end –
a sign of a driver's poor shifting technique – our mini-business would waste fuel and lose
money. Same thing if we wasted fuel by letting the engine idle too long. To make sure
we learned not do that, the engine had a recording system which detected and kept a
history of idle time and tach overspeed. Ultimately, it would affect our bonus. Similarly,
if a driver neglected maintenance, time was lost and profit, too. Engine miles were
recorded and preventive maintenance was scheduled automatically.

Schneider was one of the first companies to implement a state-of-the-art satellite
tracking and messaging system with a little satellite antenna and computer in each
tractor, common now but innovative then. At first, this controversial tracking system
upset independent-minded drivers who saw it as an invasion of privacy. It monitors
truck speed, location, ETA within minutes. When a customer tells Schneider a load is
ready to pick up, the massive computer in Green Bay knows where all 12,000 trucks are,
when they will be empty and available. The company prides itself on on-time delivery,
and if a driver is late for a just-in-time (JIT) delivery, the customer might be jeopardized
but the driver's bonus surely will be.

Wayne named a few giants: Procter and Gamble, General Motors, Lever Brothers,
Kimberly-Clark, Chrysler. In spite of tens of thousands of loads, Wayne told us
Schneider makes just ten dollars profit on each one. Takes a lot of mini-businesses at
ten bucks a load, and the company line was that it didn't take much to turn a load from
profit to loss.

Although Don Schneider inherited a union shop from his father, by the time he was
ready to grow it into the world's biggest truckload company, he created a new, non-
union Schneider National and kept his father's old union pals employed in a smaller,
sister corporation called Schneider Transport. Those union drivers have been cruising
peacefully toward retirement in an ever-shrinking company. Wayne concluded with a

pep talk about the benefits of staying non-union. "Less than truckload" freight movers like Yellow were union members, but Schneider wasn't, and aimed to keep it that way.

When Wayne finished, like clockwork we separated into two smaller groups and moved right into individual classrooms to meet our next instructor. Gary, who'd also been our morning bus driver with the bobble-head, issued each student a four-inch thick orange-and-black ring binder notebook titled "Schneider National Reference Guide." It was divided into twelve orange-tabbed sections: Emergency, Hazardous Materials, Regulatory (the thickest), Operations, Winter Reference, Pay and Benefits, Canada, etc. I flipped to "Hazardous Materials" right away and closed it right away. It looked like a chemistry book.

Gary started us going around the room introducing ourselves. We were a room full of regional accents. I recognized Kentucky and Virginia right away, got fooled by a Texan, loved the lazy, liquid Missourian who sounded like every network sports announcer. People had come from as far away as Denver and New Jersey. Elizabeth, the woman I'd smiled at earlier, was from Wisconsin and other than missing some teeth, was a cheerful, attractive woman. She mentioned she'd been laid off from the Speed Queen factory, second shift, and needed a job that would pay her what she'd been making before – $12/hour.

A guy from Tennessee who'd been working on Mississippi river barges claimed his job was the most dangerous in the world. A married man from Kentucky had a little business hauling premium hay to race horse stables. A former teacher in a Carlton College sweatshirt wanted to see the USA. But the guy we all envied because we knew he had it made was a "yard jockey" whose job had been to park semis in a warehouse lot all day.

My turn came and because I wanted to fit in and since it might sound pretentious, I decided not to say much about China or toys. Instead, I said I was self-employed and enjoyed working with my husband. Gary chuckled, "You're going to see him a whole heck of a lot now!" The whole class chuckled right along. Then he added, "My wife and I loved teaming, but then we started having kids." His wife, Val, was the instructor in the other classroom. She had hair to her waist.

David, next to me, didn't mention he was a mechanical engineer – just that he designed machinery. This was, except for a tiny number of us, a blue collar group. They'd worked at loading docks, in stores stocking shelves, driving repair trucks for stores like Sears, several were just out of the military, a handful drove fork lifts. Two recent college graduates needed a fast way to pay down debts. One had his commercial pilot's license but couldn't find a steady job.

The most intriguing guy in the circle was Mike, a giant man about sixty with a basso voice and the letters *R I G H T* tattooed on the knuckles of his right hand. He'd been working for a Milwaukee company that makes specialized trucks for hazardous waste clean-up at airports. His job was to deliver the trucks to airports around the world and teach locals how to run them. There wasn't a developed country he hadn't visited, and later we learned the reason he quit this exciting job was because he was scared to death he'd be caught in crossfire in the Lebanon or Calais airports. Lebanon was the worst, he said, followed closely by Greece.

We spent the next four days in the classroom. Right away, we learned trucking is a twenty-four hour a day business. No more eight hour days with time-and-a-half for overtime. To make the point, Schneider picked us up at 5:30 AM and dropped us back at the motel at 4:30 PM – with still hours more of written homework to do before morning. That meant getting up at 4 AM in time to have our free breakfast next door at Denny's. So much for all that breakfast food we'd hauled along.

We learned how to keep log books, stay safe, keep awake, calculate the hours left to legally drive, plan a trip (we were issued a free Rand McNally Motor Carriers' Atlas – a

$17 freebie), and 'placard' a trailer load of mercuric oxycyanide with aluminum ferrosilicon powder. We learned the theory behind downshifting on a mountain grade, adjusting the West Coast mirrors, checking oil, antifreeze, fan belt tension, the fuel-water separator, tread depth, air pressure, air brake connections, checking the four-way flashers. There was a lot to check, and every night there was a lot of trip planning homework until late at night in the motel room. We were getting exhausted and hadn't yet been within arm's length of a truck.

A four-inch binder holds a lot of material. Each day we had several exams to make sure we'd been paying attention. Our black and orange file folders filled up with dozens of exam papers. We figured this documentation would satisfy lawyers charged with defending Schneider's training program if any of us caused an accident. They could say, "Hey, we taught him not to change lanes in the middle of an intersection. Look, it's right here on his exam sheet."

It had been many years since I'd tried to memorize anything – even remembering a phone number long enough to dial it without looking is difficult for me. But our tests were open-book and easy to pass, for almost everyone, that is, except Warren, the hay hauler, whose wife and baby waited for him back in Kentucky. Warren never quite seemed to finish his test. One by one we'd hand in our tests to Gary and leave the room to grab a smoke or coffee. Warren was left to shuffle through his four-inch binder. The rest of the class would wait outside until the door re-opened, and there he'd be, still shuffling.

By Tuesday, the first day we set foot in a real truck, I was brain dead. Cramming for exams every night is okay for college kids, but I'd passed that way thirty years ago. Plus, the motel was filled with world-class smokers, and air re-circulating through our room was the same that circulated through theirs. Every morning my eyes were sore and swollen because of smoky, smoggy air.

At this point school became two very different experiences for David and me. I really couldn't understand the mechanical and technical information in the Schneider guide. I was tired, and I was dumb. I hoped whatever spunk that had gotten me this far would carry me through another week. It seemed doubtful.

But there I was, in the 5:15 dawn riding to the training center, eyes red, brain dead, not ready to drive a truck. I hoped beyond hope David would be my partner. Each driving instructor took two or three students in his truck, and I was worried about embarrassing myself in front of strangers. The instructors began to call out names. Mine came right away followed by "Jeff Carstensen." No David.

Jeff, a lanky, quiet, ragged blonde who smoked off by himself during every break, sat just a few seats away from me in Gary's classroom. He was a determined student, working through the guide, knowing his wife and young son were depending on him to get his CDL. Trip planning gave him the most trouble; he whipped through hazardous materials. We'd make a good pair.

Our instructor, A. G., reminded me instantly of my military step-father. He wore an orange and black Schneider regulation uniform, Schneider cap, spoke matter-of-factly, recited his list of expectations, smiled courteously when he finished, and told us it was time to "fire her up." I liked A. G.; I knew he wouldn't let anything bad happen to me.

We bundled up in our winter clothes, Jeff in his mittens and light nylon windbreaker, me in my new insulated bibs, down coat, scarf, wool mittens. It was 10 above zero outside. We followed A. G. out into the pitch black morning to the row of waiting bobtails (no trailers) and tractor #12661 plugged into an electrical outlet to keep the engine warm.

"Never start the engine with her plugged in," A. G. said, pulling out the plug. "Never start the engine until you do a four-point."

We'd learned the four-point inspection in class. Oil, antifreeze, fuel, and belts. There are four belts you can see when you bend down and peek behind the front wheel with a flashlight. All four belts need to be there, and none should be broken or visibly cracked. What the four belts did was something else.

The tractor itself was filthy. When the tractor is alone and not hitched up to the trailer, you're able to inspect the fifth wheel which is the large horseshoe-shaped fitting that the pin of the trailer fits into. It's normally slathered with lubricating grease so the trailer turns easily behind the tractor. But besides lubricating grease, this tractor was covered with the dregs of a long Wisconsin winter – all the road salt and dirty clods of ice and mud frozen around each of the important mechanisms we were supposed to check.

There was no way to do it. I couldn't imagine knowing for sure whether the brake chambers, for instance, really were tightly bolted to what they were supposed to be bolted to. You couldn't see the bolts. Nevertheless, A. G. methodically flashed his light at about thirty critical items we were supposed to declare safe and secure. This was part of the one-hundred-thirty-four step pre-trip-inspection. I took his word that everything worked.

Now that we finished outside, it was time to climb into the room-sized cab. This was my first trip into a cab-over. All the trucks David and I had been in were conventionals. A. G. told us how to do it. "Always start with the foot closest to the front bumper when you get into a cab. More accidents happen here than on the road. Right here is where backs get broken."

Four feet above me was the threshold of the door. Book bag over my shoulder, I clambered up one step, a second step, to the threshold, grabbing handholds as I ascended and heaved in my book bag containing the four-inch binder and flashlight. Almost there, I crawled spider-like across the seat, hurdled the gearshift and engine cover (the "dog house") and flopped onto the studio-sized mattress behind the front seats. A. G. got in the driver's seat, Jeff in the passenger's.

"Never have her in gear, always cover the brake pedal, clutch in, watch the gauges," A. G. said. I'd meant to ask earlier what "cover the brake pedal" meant, and I couldn't see past A. G. 's arm to notice what the brake pedal was doing. Maybe later. He pushed the starter button, and she fired up.

A bobtail has a nice solid roar that radiates from the carpeted dog house between the seats, so loud that you can't be heard unless you use your best crowded-bar shout. So every communication is a shout.

The inside of these school tractors was spartan, nothing like the fancy tractors David and I visited at the dealers. This one had a CB dangling down and a red light affixed to the dash. "What's that?" I shouted.

"Tells me you're in reverse when you shouldn't be," A. G. shouted back. Good, I thought. Glad someone knows.

For the next hour, A. G. demonstrated the operation of a Cummins diesel engine, Fuller transmission, and Eaton brake system. He circled the parking lot a dozen times, following behind dozens of other bobtails also circling the parking lot like a troupe of orange circus elephants.

He showed us what double-clutching involves, how air brakes behave, the turning radius of this oversized vehicle. Then he took us out for a ride to a nearby industrial park and showed us how to make a right-hand turn, how we should come to within sixty feet of the corner, set up four feet from the curb, foot off the fuel, shift into neutral, brake until the speed is reduced to eight miles an hour, watch the tachometer, rev to 1000 rpm's, shift into fourth, and gracefully execute the turn while keeping the engine below 1200 rpm's. He did this again and again like a pro. This was the classic "bump and run" turn. Not a word of it made sense to me.

"We'll take a break and then you can give it a try," he said, and I was praying he was talking to Jeff, not me. I'd tried very hard to memorize the gearshift pattern during the previous week. I'd been using the special training chairs in the motel and cafeteria that were outfitted with real Fuller gearshift simulators. Although the mechanism in the chair was only a couple of springs, it gave me a sense of where second and sixth were (the same place), third and seventh (the same place), fourth and eighth (the same place), and fifth and ninth (the same place.) High gears are actuated by the position of a plastic thumb switch lever on the gearshift knob. It's up for high gears and down for low range gears. Reverse and first gear are off to the left side of the shifting pattern, separated from the other gears by a heavy spring, so heavy I needed to use both hands. They were so far to the left that only a pumped and panicky student could get way over there by accident.

We had a short coffee break; Jeff had a cigarette, and then went back to the tractor. I held my breath. "Why don't you hop in the driver's seat, Jeff?" A. G. said, handing him the keys.

Jeff re-adjusted the air-ride seat, buckled up, and glanced at all the mirrors, of which there are six on a student-training tractor. Four are standard on all trucks; the left and right "West Coast" mirrors are the big, flat rectangles, the left and right "spot" mirrors are round and convex for a wide-angle distorted view of a large area. Just for the instructor in the passenger seat, there's a spot mirror outside the left windshield so he can see back along that side of the truck, and on cab-overs there is a spot mirror outside a little peek hole window down by the passenger's legs, supposedly for viewing the driver's "blind spot" down there. With a passenger in the seat, that peek hole is not visible.

Jeff cranked his window down and fine-tuned the two driver side mirrors, then had to talk A. G. through the adjustment of the two passenger side mirrors up, down, in, out. Remote controls for mirror adjustment were finally finding their way into only newer trucks those days, a long overdue "luxury." Satisfied with the mirrors, Jeff started the engine, put it in gear and we lurched to a stop. "That is sixth gear," said A. G. "Switch is down for low range gears like second, which is what you want."

Embarrassed, Jeff re-started the engine, tried again with the switch down and we lurched ahead a few yards until he tried to shift up to third gear. The gearbox growled but refused to mesh as we coasted to a stop. "Remember to double-clutch," A. G. said. He would remind us to do this many hundreds of times during the next two weeks.

It is not a natural thing if you're used to driving a normal, synchronized transmission on your city car. In a truck, not only do you have to clutch in, clutch out, clutch in, clutch out every time you shift, you also have to depress the clutch no further than about half way to the floor. If you depress too far, you engage the clutch brake. Whenever the gears clashed Jeff would instinctively stab the clutch clear to the floor engaging the clutch brake and making the shift impossible. A. G. said normally you don't want to engage the clutch brake. At the time I didn't know why and didn't feel this was the time to ask. I'd ask David to explain later the new term, "clutch brake."

For the next hour, we lurched and stalled and lurched and stalled in the big circular racetrack around the parking area with Jeff at the wheel. I expected more from Jeff. He was already a master of the pre-trip inspection, and I could tell he studied his big Schneider Reference Guide. Somehow I thought he'd grasped the concept of double-clutching and shifting by reading pages five and six. He was a male. This was in his genes. When his time was up, I could tell he wasn't happy with his performance. He'd clutched.

"So," A. G. said as he turned his friendly face back to me where I was lodged defensively into the mattress. "Ready?"

I really was not ready. I really did not want to do this. After the trouble Jeff had, I was convinced this, in driving terms, was the road to ruin. Intellectually, I didn't understand the concept of shifting so translating it into action was doomed. To make matters worse, this wasn't going to be a private failure. I had two observers.

I climbed across the gearshift and sat behind the wheel. Jeff got onto the mattress and strapped himself in. A. G. hadn't moved. I fiddled with the air-ride seat and the mirrors. I started the engine using the prescribed procedure in the guide.

And then it was hell.

I had no idea what to do, what I'd just done, where to find any gear at any given moment, how to look simultaneously at the speedometer, the tachometer, four mirrors and straight ahead like some idiot bobble-head. Nothing in life had prepared me for this.

A. G. betrayed nothing. No displeasure, no anxiety, no anger, no hate. He just sat there, lurching along with us, repeating again and again, "Watch your rpm's. Where's second gear? What gear are you in? What gear do you want to be in? What's your speed? What gear are you in? What's the speed for fourth gear? Have you memorized pages five and six in your reference guide? What gear are you looking for? Look where the clutch pedal is. (It was clear to the floor.) What speed do you want for sixth? Watch your rpm's. You're in reverse. Watch them rpm's."

Not to mention the accelerator. The accelerator pedal, I announced, was broken. If you merely touched it with your foot, the engine rpm's raced dangerously to 2200 and above. This was bad for our mini-business. This was far above the normal operating range for the heavy, expensive Cummins engine. The engine turbo charger screamed and whined. You couldn't miss it when your rpm's were out of control. Nonetheless, how can you actually do something about it when you're watching the tachometer and speedometer and traffic and doing math calculations in your head trying to make the best of nine different gear choices for 1,000 rpm at 35 mph.

Clad in warm hiking boots for this inaugural day of driving and buffered by the heavy sole of my accelerator foot, just touching the sensitive pedal would race the engine and make it whine. The tiniest kinesthetic spasm could move the tachometer into over-speed territory.

I was learning firsthand about the term, "It rides like a truck." Truck springs are made to carry a fully-loaded 80,000 pounds. Our empty tractor bounced like it had no springs. Each bounce further aggravated the throttle problem by syncopating foot and pedal action. I tried to compensate by rubbing the right side of my boot against the wall of the carpeted engine compartment using friction to keep my foot resting gently on the hair-trigger throttle.

I hate to whine, but the pedal designers used the identically shaped part to make both the throttle pedal and the brake pedal. They thought it would be convenient just to slide a foot from one to the other, but instead they'd made it possible to apply both at the same time if your warm hiking boots crossed the crack between them.

We broke for lunch. Inside the cafeteria, there were few smiles. I found David. "How's it going?" he asked. He didn't wait for my answer and said instead, "This is the hardest thing I've ever tried to do. Compared to this, Air Force jet pilot training was child's play."

Gone was David's macho look. Now he looked worried. "I'm not kidding," he said. "This is hard. Peace time military training can afford to go slow – it was four months before we saw the inside of a cockpit. Schneider's got us in these trucks in four days. I suppose they know what they're doing because a ton of drivers graduate. Very few wash out." I knew he was trying to make me feel better.

He went on. "Nobody in my truck could do squat, especially Bobbie," he said. "She's hopeless. Raced the engine every goddamn time. And I'm afraid she's not strong enough to pull out the fifth wheel handle."

My heart went out to Bobbie. She was the blonde, weathered woman who came to Green Bay with her boyfriend. He had his CDL and was just here to be 'Schneiderized,' but she was a rookie student just like me. She'd been a security guard for Samsonite in Denver, knew how to open up the back door of a semi and look inside for smuggled goods, but that was it. She quit that perfectly good job to try this.

She and her boyfriend planned to go back to Denver and "work the system" when she graduated. They'd pick up and deliver anywhere in the states or Canada. David and I were going to be "dedicated" Kimberly-Clark drivers. At this point, everybody's dreams were looking more and more unrealistic, maybe hopeless.

"Is your accelerator particularly sensitive?" I asked.

"No."

"I don't think I can do this." There, I'd said it again. We'd talked about our plans for months, absolutely determined to change our lives and live a new dream, and I was already talking about pulling the plug.

5

B ack at the motel that night, David tried desperately to teach me the mechanics of driving. We acknowledged the problems of an unforgiving 9-speed transmission, 2-stage clutch, air brakes, brake pedal identical to the accelerator pedal, huge mirrors on both sides to block your side vision, and no rear window. But the overriding difficulty for everyone, himself included, was shifting the 9-speed.

Stick shift car transmissions, he explained, are loaded with delicate and expensive brass friction rings called synchronizers that mesh the various gears just before a shift. This helps prevent gear "grinding". But a truck transmission has to last a million miles and 9, 10, 15, even 18 gear speeds are commonly used to help a reasonably-sized engine accelerate the huge loads in big trucks. To eliminate the maintenance nightmare, synchronizers have been eliminated. It's up to the driver to "double clutch" the shifting procedure to overcome this omission. That is, clutch and shift into neutral, let up the clutch pedal and tap the accelerator to spin the engine a little above where it would be spinning if you were already in the next gear at the current wheel speed, then tap the clutch and quickly select your next gear at the moment the engine rpm falls past the perfect mesh speed. Real-men drivers do the routine up and down shifts without using the clutch at all. With or without, it all depends on perfect rpm control and timing.

Starting out in second gear and accelerating steadily by double-clutching up through third, fourth, fifth, et cetera to ninth is not too bad. Also, going to neutral and coming to a stop with the brakes is easy. The problem comes when, from high speed, you go into neutral while braking toward a stop light and bingo! The light turns green while you're still going, say, 25 mph.

There you are, in neutral at 25 mph. What's the right gear and engine rpm for accelerating from 25 up toward 55mph? What if this happens while you're going down hill? Going up hill? For each speed there are three gear choices depending on whether you want to be in gear at a high rpm (for power or decelerating), medium rpm (for cruising), or low rpm (for coasting or accelerating).

We didn't use reverse or low gear on the streets, so that left second through ninth, eight different gears times three speeds for each, twenty-four unique situations. That was clearly too many to memorize. The key is to memorize only the correct cruising speed for each gear at medium engine rpm. With that mastered, you can choose a gear one step lower (high rpm) for more power and for slowing down. Or you can choose a gear one step higher (low rpm) when speeding up.

Just to keep it interesting, there is a brake – the clutch brake – on the engine half of the transmission that stops it from spinning when you need a gear at zero miles per hour, like at a stop sign. Even with the clutch in, unless there's a clutch brake, there is enough friction in the clutch to keep the engine gears spinning too much to shift at a dead stop. The clutch brake is applied by pushing the clutch pedal all the way to the floor. Every new driver has to learn that if he makes the gears grind in a shift at 20 miles per hour, the cure is not to push harder on the clutch pedal. That only makes the gear rpm mismatch even worse (20 mph wheels, zero rpm engine gear). Double-clutch technique must only use the top half of the clutch pedal travel. Any over-travel is counterproductive, causes premature wear on the $2,000 clutch brake, and leaves you coasting to a stop in neutral halfway through an intersection.

I really hated the frigging clutch brake.

Because we practiced as bobtails, without the length and weight of a trailer attached, there was way too much power and brake capacity. Add to this the bouncy ride (no trailer weight on the springs) in a driver's seat that is free to bounce up, down, forward and backward, you needed fine-tuned physical control, and that was impossible. The only thing similar in the Air Force is instrument flying through clouds, but David pointed out that you get simulator time and several months to learn it. This is a two week school with only about seven driving days and two or three hours per day of actual driving per student.

By the end of the second day in the truck, A. G. was losing confidence, too. While some of the other teams had already coupled to a trailer, Jeff and I were still bobtailing around the industrial park. Jeff was clearly making progress. He could do a flawless "bump and run," a term for downshifting into an appropriate gear before turning the corner. To do it right, you make a judgment about which gear to use before you get to the corner – usually third or fourth for a right-hand turn, and fourth or fifth for a left-hand turn. You slow down to six mph for third gear, eight mph for fourth gear, or ten mph for fifth and clutch into neutral without engaging the clutch brake. You "bump" – revving up to 1000 rpm's – no more, no less and select the range level for the gear – sixth and above are high and the rest were low. Range level is activated by switching up or down a little up/down switch on the gearshift handle. Then you clutch into the proper gear without engaging the clutch brake, turn the corner and "run" – accelerating slowly but steadily through the turn so as to keep the mirrors from shaking.

All the while, you are supposed to be "setting up" for the turn which means, for a right hand turn, staying four feet from the curb (so your trailer, when you have one, won't jump up over it), and activating the turn signals. This narrow space discourages all but bicycles and motorcycles from squeezing into your "blind side" and being squished when you turn the corner. Or, for a left-hand turn, you line up along the centerline. And of course, you're looking for traffic everywhere, deciding how far into the intersection to go to so your trailer tandems don't "off-track" and obliterate a stop sign, light pole, person, car, dog, concrete island, etc. Since we were still bobtailing, these off-tracking details mattered little.

Still, bump and runs were impossible for me. Not once did I do it right. I renamed them "bump and grinds."

Despite humiliating lack of progress with shifting, we stayed on schedule for the third day and hooked a 48-foot semi-trailer to our tractor for loops around the parking lot and through the industrial neighborhood. This added attraction, although visually impressive, even intimidating, was not such a big deal. A. G. demonstrated a wide right turn called a "buttonhook" which momentarily puts the tractor far into the left lane and oncoming traffic. It's designed to keep from cutting over the right corner with the trailer wheels, and you have to watch the end of the trailer in your convex mirror every single second until you've finished the turn.

As for seeing much of anything in a spot mirror, it's like looking at fun house mirrors at the carnival. Everything's distorted, in a strange perspective, unreadable to the uninitiated. The big flat West Coast mirrors provide a big, undistorted view of everything straight back behind the cab. But as soon as the truck makes a sharp turn, the West Coast mirrors can't see the tailgate anymore. They are still focused straight back along the cab but the trailer is articulated way off to the side. You have to switch your gaze to the spot mirrors, big fish eyes that see a wide-angle view of everything, but greatly distorted.   So distorted, it was pretty much meaningless at my stage of development, not helpful in predicting the course of travel for trailer tandems.   I depended on A. G.   If he stayed quiet, I was pretty sure nothing bad was about to happen back there.

I wasn't ready for buttonhooks anyway. I still came to dead stops in the middle of the street.   Each time the engine killed, it nicked a little more self-esteem off my dwindling supply and added anxiety to the next turn and the next, eventually becoming the classic self-fulfilling prophecy.

I discovered that the only way for me to even begin to negotiate a turn was to talk it through out loud. Some of what I said was elementary Dick and Jane. I asked A. G. if he minded this talking. "Oh no," he said. "'Commentary driving' is acceptable." There was even a word for it.

I faked insouciance. "Now Shelley," I'd say to the passengers in the truck, "there's a left-hand turn half a block ahead. You'll need to slow down . . . slow down . . . *slow* down (and I'd start braking), and now, you need to choose a gear – how about fifth? Fifth is good. You've always liked fifth gear. Oh god, here comes a car (and a car would appear in the lane I planned to use to make my turn), and let's see now, where is fifth gear? I see that car. Ah yes, fifth gear is upper right in the gearshift pattern, and what gear am I in now? Shit, I can't remember which gear I'm in (and I couldn't), so let's check how fast I'm going (and I'd take my eyes off the approaching car and study the speedometer), looks like fifteen miles an hour, so I must be in sixth or seventh gear, which is it?" A. G. offered no help. He didn't laugh. He didn't smile.

Meanwhile the intersection was at hand.   We had by then graduated to lightly-traveled city streets.   In fact, we were moving steadily through the intersection, and one of several things would happen: the light would change; an on-coming car would signal for a left-turn in front of me; the engine would stall; we'd come to a full stop and have to start off in second gear; I'd forget to flip the low-range selector button for second, so instead of starting off in second, I'd be trying to start off in sixth from a dead stop, and that just doesn't work; someone would honk at the stalled truck in the intersection; A. G. would say, "What gear are you in?"

I'd been here before – in tenth grade plane geometry. Nothing penetrated that prison of confusion I was in after the first week of plane geometry. I tried to measure the angles right off the textbook diagram with my steel compass praying that one would match the answer in the back of the book. It never worked. Like David struggled to do the night before, my father, a civil engineer, tried to explain theorems and no matter how hard I tried, nothing clicked. Nothing about shifting clicked either, and I felt myself losing it.

Physically, my fingers were locked around the steering wheel for so long that, once unwrapped, they wouldn't relax. Tennis elbow, which came from chipping ice on our Wisconsin driveway, returned. My right leg shook uncontrollably because of overwork on the brake at inclines. I was so terrified I'd roll back and flatten something behind me that I'd keep the brake pedal plastered to the floor until the light changed. And now pulling a 20,000 pound trailer hooked on the back, the temperamental throttle needed to be floored just to get a little head of steam to thirty-five miles per hour. Plus it was so damn cold that every time we had to take our gloves off to check oil, or drain the water in the fuel-water separator, my fingers which had been frost-bitten fifteen years earlier cross country skiing, reminded me how stupid it was to be in Green Bay in the dead of winter.

Coupled with all this, it was sobering that for the first time in my educational experience I couldn't count on being measured against the curve. In high school and college, it was generally not a problem to squeeze a decent grade out of a course because although never the smartest, I was usually not the dumbest and would land somewhere in the middle of the bell curve, except for descriptive linguistics which I failed flat out. That wasn't the case here at trucking school. No hiding in the curve; either you learned to shift and to back up or you were out.

For some in the class, the downfall wouldn't be the mechanics of driving – maybe they'd been yard jockeys for a warehouse somewhere in Iowa for the last ten years, shuttling trailers from one end of the lot to the other all day. They knew how to back a 53' trailer into a deep, dark narrow hole blindfolded. Their Waterloo might be map reading – they'd never been out of Iowa, never planned a trip past Waterloo, never even used a map and Schneider would fail them if they couldn't find the quickest, cheapest route into the rusty core of Detroit.

After four days in the truck, David suggested I try a new instructor. He assured me this kind of thing happened all the time in Air Force flight school. There was even a formal procedure for it. Reacting, I'm sure, to my dreary nightly recaps, he smelled failure coming.

I'm the kind of person who has to learn things in sequence, to understand each step in the process before taking the next one. So, really, I wasn't learning anything anymore. I'd missed the first step. Nothing was intuitive – the mechanical, the physical, the spatial was all being "learned" from scratch and at a pace that ignored my special need to take it one slow, tedious step at a time, and once mastered, take the next step. A. G. kept saying things like, "We can't go back over the same stuff day after day. We don't have time to re-learn everything. Trust the training. Let's move forward." But that's not how I learned. Like getting lost in a maze, I had to go back to a well-known landmark and start from there.

I kept resisting David's new instructor suggestion because it was too awkward to confront A. G. On the fourth day A. G. dropped me off at the motel and went out solo with Jeff because Jeff showed promise, and I was holding him back. After lunch it would be my turn, ready at last for lonely, county roads pulling a 48' trailer. I spent the morning in the motel with ice cubes from the vending machine wrapped in a wash cloth and balanced on my head. The amaryllis bud revealed a little red. It was medicine on an otherwise bleak day in Green Bay in February, but not enough to keep me from seriously re-thinking the whole trucking idea.

A. G. picked me up and moved into the passenger seat. This, I figured, was my last chance to do it right. Following A. G.'s directions, we headed out of Green Bay, up Hwy. 41 to the lonely, county road. My headache was better. I was ready to learn, churning up whatever lay in a diminished reservoir of resolve.

"You'll have plenty of room out here to practice your downshifting, no one in your way." A. G. was always calmly matter-of-fact. "Turn right on County D up ahead."

County roads are narrow. I practiced centering the 102" wide tractor-trailer in my lane. The large, flat West Coast mirrors showed the wheels had about 12" leeway on either side between shoulder and center line. It's easy to spend more time looking backward than forward at times like this.

I heard A. G. say, "Turn left at the next intersection." It loomed several hundred feet ahead. No cars anywhere. I signaled left. I edged over to the centerline. I calculated we were in ninth gear doing forty-five and had to get to fourth gear somehow. I slowed to eight miles an hour, clutched into neutral, revved to 1000, clutched into fourth and began my left turn. It was a perfect bump and run.

"*Stop! Stop! Stop!*" A. G. screamed. I stood on the air brakes and came to a full stop. The tractor was already well into the turn and the trailer was diagonal across the oncoming lane.

"Read that sign!" he commanded.

An insignificant white sign on a post stood twenty-five feet up the road ahead on the shoulder. I read out loud.

"Class B trucks only." I withered – we were Class A.

"You can't go down this road. *Back up!*"

This was unbelievable. "You're kidding," I said. "You told me to turn left."

"No, I told you to turn right."

"But I was signaling for a left turn the whole time. My set-up was for a left turn," I insisted.

A. G. didn't say anything. He jumped out of the cab and came around to my side. He was angry.

"Put on your four-way flashers and do *exactly* what I tell you."

Meanwhile, an oncoming car appeared, stopped and was watching this whole fiasco.

"Put it in reverse." I remembered the page in the reference guide that said "Never back into a public road." I couldn't believe this was happening to me.

"Turn left. More left! Slowly. Now right. Slowly! Keep going."

I could see another car pulling up behind me. I kept following A. G.'s instructions until I was backed up on my side of the road. There were about six cars watching this whole thing now. About four minutes had elapsed. He got back in.

"Turn right at the next intersection."

By now there was a car waiting at the intersection, watching.

"There's not enough room," I said. "I'll hit that car."

"Do a modified buttonhook."

I'd never done a buttonhook of any kind, just watched A. G. in the industrial park. Now I had no choice. I eased into my first buttonhook, and mercifully, the car waiting at the stop sign backed up to make room.

This was my first experience with how car drivers can make a huge difference to truck drivers. If this driver hadn't been able or inclined to back up a few feet (luckily there wasn't another car behind him), I simply couldn't have made this tight turn. It would have been a stalemate. If I'd tried to make the turn without his backing up, the tandems (the back wheels of the trailer) would have off-tracked into a three-foot-wide drainage ditch. Until you're sitting behind the wheel of an 18-wheeler, you cannot appreciate this. But this nice car driver, by backing up, allowed me enough room to keep all the parts of the tractor-trailer on the pavement.

Meanwhile, A. G. wasn't speaking. I wasn't either. In fact, I was really pissed at him. Why the hell didn't he see my turn signal for a left, not right turn? I think he may have been thinking the same thing, because, except for this lapse, A. G. knew exactly what kind of trouble I was getting myself into in every one of the other dozens of awful situations. But not this time. In my mind at this minute, it was time to forget driving and try something else.

That night as I relived the afternoon's meltdown, David insisted that tomorrow we would ask for a new instructor. He wanted to switch with me – he'd take A. G. and I'd take Rick, who'd been working one-on-one with Bobbie, sometimes for six-hour stretches. Measured by his students' graduation rate and subsequent longevity with Schneider, Rick Glazer was the star of the group of sixty instructors. It was clear why. He grew up on a farm north of Green Bay, drove trucks right out of high school, married his high school sweetheart (now a Schneider accounts payable employee), owned two of his own trucks for a while, and at the age of thirty-nine started training Schneider recruits. His personality and values were perfect for the job. He told David about one couple who required four weeks of his personal attention to get through the two-week course. He took them to an empty industrial park one Sunday and had them run the truck backward around a warehouse parking lot for a full day until they got the hang of it. That couple was one of his triumphs, hauling steadily for Schneider ever since.

First thing the next morning while it was still dark in Green Bay, we walked into the training center and met A. G.

I'd rehearsed my short speech. "A. G.," I said. "Have I got a deal for you. David and I would like to switch places. You take David, who is very good, and I'll take Rick, David's instructor."

A. G. stood there speechless, not a hint of compassion in his face.

"Are you saying you want to switch instructors?"

"I think it's worth a try," I said.

He stood there. I stood there with David by my side. I loved David very much for being with me.

"David is a great student. You'll like him," I said cheerily.

"You want a new instructor?"

We stood there pondering the lobby carpet.

"Okay. This will take some work, but we'll get you a new instructor." A. G. didn't follow up on my wanting the known quantity, Rick. I was afraid to push it.

He disappeared and David was beckoned away by Rick. They were going to the truck along with Bobbie and Keith, their third driving partner. I stood alone in the hall for about twenty minutes feeling like a truant. A. G. came back and said, "Okay, it took a lot of shuffling, but I've got you a new instructor."

Clearly, it wasn't going to be Rick because he'd already left.

I was ushered into a "One on One" room. A. G. closed the door, sat down, pulled out all the sheets of evaluation papers he'd shown me a day or so before. "See," he said, pointing to a column of skills I should have mastered by now. "You're progressing in this, this, and this. The only thing you have to work on is shifting. You *think* too much. Just trust the training. Remember what I tell you and trust the training."

This was official military talk. I grew up with a military father who told war stories about soldiers going into combat for the first time. They were taught to trust the training; just jump from the goddamn plane and you'll automatically grab the rip-cord.

I decided to argue with the officer. "It's not that I don't trust the training, A. G. I can't shift the goddamn truck. Your training goes too fast for me. You're asking me to do things that require I understand the basics. I don't understand the basics. This is all new to me. I come *tabula rasa.*"

He didn't know "*tabula rasa.*"

The door opened and my new instructor appeared. He was an olive-complexioned man with black, curly hair, wore aviator glasses, and had extra lines in his cheeks. He looked like a clean-cut Harley driver, and later I learned that's exactly what he was.

"This is Harry," A. G. said. Then he turned to me and said, "Now let me ask you something, Shelley. Do you really want to learn how to drive? Wasn't this your husband's idea?"

This was a stunning question. Both men were dead silent.

I thought for a moment. "Believe it or not, I came up with this crazy idea. Certainly I want to learn how to drive. I study the reference guide until my eyes cross, I am earnest about this, and of course, I want to learn how to drive. Why? What makes you think I don't?"

"So, are you frightened?" Harry asked.

"Well, I think it's safe to say I'm respectful of how little I know, how big the truck is, and how I'm being asked to do things before I'm ready. But I wouldn't say I'm frightened. Why? Do I seem frightened?"

This line of questioning reminded me of another introduction several years earlier. It was a new job, first day, with a small company called "Earth Care Paper" in Madison. It was my first job since Pleasant Company (now The American Girls), and although I'd vowed never to work again after such an (excuse me) unpleasant experience, I found myself eagerly hired by Earth Care as their marketing manager. So, I was surprised to be ushered aside to a small conference room on that first day accompanied by the young owner and his wife and the personnel manager. "We have learned over the weekend," Carol said ill-humoredly, speaking for the group, "that you were a difficult employee at Pleasant Company. Could you tell us about that?"

I wondered who'd tattled. Well, the truth was I was a difficult employee. I tended to disagree with Pleasant, not an endearing trait in an employee, and I was frugal to a fault and ridiculously practical, something Pleasant wasn't. I never did learn the art of sucking up. So I explained my side of the story and told Carol and John I'd be happy to show them Pleasant's glowing letter of recommendation. They were satisfied, but I forever resented the way they mishandled what should have been a warm welcome on my first day of work. Where was the mug of coffee and hearty handshake, anyway? Through no fault of my own, they went bankrupt a year after I'd left. And divorced each other, too.

So here I was again, feeling a little unwelcome at trucking school and a little persecuted by my old instructor. The meeting ended and it was time to test-drive Harry.

What a difference just the tiniest sense of humor makes. Harry could laugh. The first morning out with Harry and my new driving partner, Jay, was an instant success. Not that I could suddenly shift, but there was something about how Harry lay back in the passenger seat, foot up on the dash, easy laugh, gentle kidding that made all the difference in the world. His relaxed attitude, unlike A. G.'s, didn't trigger an adrenaline rush when I flubbed a gear. He was my kind of teacher.

And at last, there was real progress. Finally the principle of matching the gears to the revolutions of the engine made sense and with it several correct bump and runs all in one day. With enough practice, maybe it would start to be instinctual. That's how it was for Jay, a delightful thirty-year old from Virginia, who was already a pretty good shifter. The only thing he didn't do right was listen to Harry tell him where to turn. We'd sail by the intersection, Jay smiling the whole way, yabbering in his special Virginia liquid drawl.

Week two goals were to get through skid-pad training, parking, and more importantly, through the CDL road test– the driving portion of the commercial driver's license. Several Schneider instructors were licensed third-party CDL testers for the DOT, so the test was given right there on the Schneider lot. Cones for the straight backing maneuver and 45-degree angle backing were just beyond the pull-through slots where we parked our trailers after class. Backing into a parking spot – instead of pulling through – was saved for the later stages of training, a measure of the special challenge it presents.

"You're scheduled for skid pad Tuesday afternoon," Harry said to me first thing Monday. "You'll be ready."

I'm not sure how a person got ready for skid pad. David was no help; he hadn't done it yet. Skid pad is nothing but a big smooth blacktop parking lot and a fire hose. We'd been watching all week as everyone got their turn to race across the huge ice-covered lot in a special flat-bed and later in a bobtail, slam on the brakes, spin wildly out of control in a series of full turns and a cloud of spray, and land upright against the snow bank at the other end. To date, no one had died. The only injury was a sore shoulder when a bobtail hit a bunch of deep ruts at the far end and bounced the student around a little. Our Schneider recruitment video didn't mention injuries.

Big tractors are not top heavy. The cab is lightweight aluminum and fiberglass construction; the frame, engine and wheels make up most of the weight which is relatively close to the ground. Tractors only tip over if coupled to a tall trailer that tips over. The flatbed trailer was a good choice. Chains welded to the sides of the flatbed and its tractor made it a special jack-knife proof rig. It wasn't unusual to see veteran

Schneider drivers make use of this fantastic training aid to hone their skid control skills. These skills weren't the kind of thing you wanted to perfect on an icy interstate.

Prior to actual skid pad, we met with a specialist trainer to see another harrowing video which showed trailer wheel skids, drive wheel skids and steer wheel skids. Each is unique and handled differently. The only procedure in common is to stay "off the throttle, off the brake, and clutch in." The direction to steer depends on the type of skid – you counter-steer in a trailer wheel skid and steer with the direction of the skid (until you regain control) in a drive or steer wheel skid.

Our specialist explained how we'd practice skid recovery, how quick braking or accelerating on an exit or entrance ramp curve starts a skid and leads abruptly to an ugly spin-out. We'd also snake our way through a slalom course of cones at relatively high speed to practice quick, tight maneuvers. At the end of this last event stood a special plastic cone named "Grandma." The object was not to kill her.

Two bobtails and one flatbed rig were parked outside, engines running. Eight of us waited our turn, alternating between the flatbed and bobtails. I was in the first flatbed group. I walked out to the rig, got in and was greeted by a specialist sitting in the passenger seat cradling a little electrical control panel in his lap.

"Tighten your seatbelt and get ready for a wild ride," he grinned. "Are you ready?" I nodded. "Then let's go. Head down track "A" in fifth gear, accelerate as fast as you can, aim for the yellow diamond sign at the far end, and we'll see what happens!"

Whoopee!

So I accelerated as fast as I could, about 35 mph although it felt like 65, headed for the yellow diamond sign, and as soon as I got a bead on it, the specialist yelled, "Changed my mind. Head for the blue diamond." And he flipped a switch that locked up the drive wheels.

This sent us into an immediate spin and just like in the video, by aggressively steering back toward the place I wanted to go – the yellow diamond – with no throttle, no brakes and clutch in, it was possible – just barely – to bring the rig under control. We did it twice more, and each time the big, exaggerated steering movements seemed to work.

The bobtail was quite another matter. Without the ballast of the trailer hanging off the back, a bobtail has very little traction. It says all over the reference guide that, contrary to popular opinion, if you're bobtailing, allow twice as much following distance between you and the vehicle ahead because it takes longer to stop. A truck is sprung for heavy loads on hard, 100 psi tires. If empty, the tires bounce and don't make a big flat friction spot in contact with the road. You can stop a loaded truck quicker than an empty one. What's more, normal acceleration can make a bobtail's drive wheels spin if the pavement's the least bit slippery, even just wet.

Pavement on the skid pad was super slippery; it was ice. With my bobtail spin specialist giving me instructions, we careened around the corner of the "tight radius" track and spun predictably out of control. To recover from this spin, you do an unnatural thing – you steer towards the ditch or shoulder or whatever you're trying like mad to avoid. This puts the steer wheels back in line with the rest of the wheels and allows you to regain traction and control. The minute you feel the road under your seat again, you steer in the direction you want to go.

We did this four times, racing around the track, spinning out of control, regaining control. For our final trick, we accelerated across the entire distance of the pad toward the yellow diamond. Without the weight of the trailer to keep us tracking, when the specialist changed his mind about which diamond to head for and simultaneously pushed a special little brake button to start the skid, we did three high-speed, full turns throwing up huge rooster tails of spray before jerking to a backwards stop. Just like I was supposed to, I used no throttle, no brake, and no clutch, but no way was it possible to recover this extreme skid. We were out of control. It was a sobering lesson. I could have done this all day, but my turn was nearly over. We slalomed through the cone course without killing Grandma and headed back to the line of waiting students.

We pulled up in front of the training center where the entire busload of new recruits was standing outside gaping at the skid pad and me. They watched me climb down out of the bobtail and stroll nonchalantly across the parking lot in my Wall's. Grown men looked me over. I gave the crowd a thumbs-up. And added, too shyly for words, "It's a blast."

6

Back at the motel that night, David was draped on the bed watching a movie. He was wearing a brand new black and orange Schneider hat, a sure sign he'd passed his CDL.

"Missed sixteen points," he said as I walked in. "They got me for having my thumbs hooked over the steering wheel, going two feet past a stop sign before coming to a full stop, and a couple other things." He was obviously pleased with himself.

So David could be a truck driver now. I was pretty sure I needed at least an extra week to get ready for the big test. I couldn't back into a parking place, and my shifting, in spite of steady improvement, wasn't foolproof. I'd still lose gears at the most awkward times in the most conspicuous places, like downtown Green Bay. And Harry caught me once changing lanes in an intersection, a traffic violation for either a car or truck. I'd spent my whole four-wheel driving life changing lanes in intersections. I had no idea this was a violation, and it was a hard habit to break.

Tuesday morning, Harry met Jay and me in the training center cafeteria.

"Morning," he said, grinning a little. "Your CDL is scheduled Thursday morning."

That was two days away. I calculated how many more hours of practice I could squeeze in. By the time we'd examined the truck every morning for the one-hundred-thirty-four possible defects, coupled up to our trailer, done a "pump down" (air brake test), and driven into the breaking dawn, Jay and I had only about two and a half hours each of real driving time. Lunch hour was always spent on the road somewhere, often in the country at a truck stop, where the instructors would sit around and gab. The students, meanwhile, at their separate table were always itching to get back to driving.

I knew I wouldn't be ready by Thursday, but Harry could read my mind. "Yes, you will," he said.

"I can't back up," I whined.

"We'll practice today, more tomorrow. It'll come."

It's reassuring when someone believes in you, but Harry's faith was misplaced. Backing up into a parking space is tough. I'd been traumatized in 1979 when David asked me to back up the boat trailer to a boat launch ramp while he drove the motor boat around to meet me. It was only two blocks from our house, and I made such a mess of it that I got out of the car, unhitched the trailer, and muscled the thing a half block by hand to the ramp. Couldn't muscle a 48' trailer.

That afternoon with Harry standing inches from the truck's open window, the trailer pointed at an angle toward the slot between the cones, four-way flashers going, in reverse gear, I tried to remember all the little ditties about backing. There was "Righter, tighter; lefter, looser." There was "Move the top of the steering wheel in the opposite direction you want the back of the trailer to go." There was "Push the front of the trailer with the tractor, and follow the trailer with the tractor." There was "Make a series of small corrections." There was "Never make a correction until you see how you're tandems line up with the hole." There was "Never judge where the back of the trailer is until you fix the position of your tandems." There was "Steer toward the mirrors to straighten the trailer." There was "Avoid a blind-side back." And there was "Toot before you back unless you'll disturb sleeping drivers."

Bass fishermen should think about being truck drivers. Bass fishermen show off by backing their metallic sparkle bass boat trailers into tight places while all the other bass fishermen pretend not to look. They say backing a short boat trailer is much more difficult than backing a big long truck trailer, but you couldn't prove it by me.

I tooted. I backed until I could see the trailer tandems.

"Turn right!" Harry said. *"Now!"*

I checked my mirror to see if the right turn would get me tighter to my side of the hole. Nothing happened.

"Hard right!" Harry said. So much for tiny corrections.

It went on like this. Harry was actually driving this truck; I was just his inside-the-cab robot. It was Jay's turn. Jay didn't need coaching. He backed right into the hole with a single pull-up correction. Jay was a genius.

Straight backing was a different challenge, and for me, a piece of cake. Finally, here was something I could master. I felt it in my bones; it was intuitive, and I never failed to do it right. In straight backing, I practiced the little ditty, "To straighten the trailer, steer toward the mirror that has the trailer's reflection." It really works. When the left side of the trailer edged into the left mirror, all you did to straighten it out was turn the top of the wheel a little left and the left edge would disappear from the left mirror and the trailer would appear in the right mirror. I think I could back straight for half a mile if I had to. The CDL required only a hundred feet.

When Jay finished, we parked the truck by the training center and went in for a break. Bobbie followed me in from outside. She beckoned.

"Come to the bathroom with me," she said.

I hardly knew Bobbie at all, but David had heard that with only three days left to go, Bobbie found a note on her pillow from her future driving partner. He'd turned down the Schneider job offer and split for Denver without saying good-bye. With Rick's one-on-one help, she was trying her hardest to keep going.

"I lost it today," she said as the bathroom door closed behind us. She dashed into a stall, and I could hear her crying and yards of toilet paper unrolling.

"It happens to me everyday," I said, hoping she'd understand she wasn't alone.

"No I mean it. I completely lost it, just broke down sobbing in the middle of an intersection."

"I know the feeling." I knew the feeling.

"I'm giving myself until tomorrow morning. Rick's worked his head off with me, and I still forget every damn thing he's taught me." I knew this feeling.

Besides me, Bobbie and Elizabeth were the only two women left from the original five. The woman who planned to drive tankers had disappeared, and the Canadian woman driver who'd come to be 'Schneider-ized' sailed through and left. Elizabeth always smiled and chatted with the guys, still enjoying the program. But Bobbie wasn't.

Next morning she stood in the motel lobby waiting for the van back to Denver while the rest of us boarded the bus to school. Rick maintained to the end that she could have made it, and told her so, but she apparently decided it was an uphill climb too steep for her solo horsepower. And, as predicted, she never was strong enough to pull the fifth-wheel handle.

Shortly after Bobbie, another student, Warren from Kentucky, washed out. I felt particularly guilty about this because Warren was originally Harry's student but was traded to A. G. when I asked to switch instructors. Poor Warren. He'd finally passed his open-book tests but couldn't make it on the road.

I was curious about Warren. He drove a straight truck delivering hay to race horse stables. It was his own business, and he needed to keep owning this small operation until someone else bought it. Until then, his wife was counting on him to make big money as a truck driver. For Warren, as for many of the people at truck driving school, this was a dream bargain. Free school and a career in four weeks. But side-businesses were strictly against Schneider rules.

"Don't think you'll have time for that little business of yours," the instructor chuckled. "Don't think you'll have time for anything but driving a truck for Schneider. Those are company rules."

But Warren, now it appeared, had all the time in the world for delivering hay. When I saw Jeff, my old partner in A. G.'s truck, I asked him what happened.

"Well, A. G. came down real hard," Jeff said. "Told Warren that if he didn't memorize the gear speeds and rpm's, he might as well not come back in the afternoon. And to make matters worse, first time out with A. G., Warren was pulling back into the Schneider driveway and drove right up over the snow bank, nearly took down the chain link fence. He never could remember he was pulling a trailer . . . just figured he was bobtailing the whole time." He added seriously, "Warren was dangerous to himself."

I felt that way, too, about myself. I honestly believed I could back over a person without knowing it, or cruise through town obliviously wiping out telephone poles. In my mind there was no question whatsoever about the danger, and just like a teenager with her first license, I figured I'd sacrifice something during the learning curve – a bumper, a right door, maybe worse. David's kids and my kids had all had their share of early learning experiences after being licensed by the state to practice driving a car. I honestly wondered how the city of Green Bay felt being practiced on by idiots like me every day of the year. Did Schneider contribute to highway repair and maintenance in any substantial way?

Thursday morning followed a sleepless Wednesday night. I woke up at two and again at three and got up at four to shower, eat a grapefruit, read one more time though the one-hundred-thirty-four step pre-trip inspection procedure, to review the diagrams for forty-five degree backing, double-check the downshifting rpm's, the laws about stopping before railroad tracks. I knew I'd be tested on railroad tracks which you cross many times in Green Bay. Every time we did, Harry would remind us it's against state law to shift while any part of the truck is on the track. And it's best not to cross too fast and bounce his clipboard off the dash.

About the only thing I couldn't consistently do on this route was a bump and run for a left-hand turn on a particular hill near the training center. Every time I tried it, I missed the gears. I hoped to hell that was not part of the test route.

The test began at eight o'clock, so from five-fifteen until seven, Harry had me out on the lot practicing backing. He'd invested so much in my passing this test that I really hated to disappoint him. We were using the DOT set-up, so if I could master it in the next couple hours, maybe I could nail it on the test. Nobody was around. After two almost-perfect forty-five degree backs, it was time to quit. There existed a slim possibility I could pass this part of the CDL.

Val was my CDL tester, part of the third party DOT testing team. She was the attractive, hair-to-the-waist, ex-trucker and the wife of Gary, our first classroom teacher. He met her waitressing in a Texas truck stop, taught her how to drive his big truck, and they married and teamed until they had children a few years ago. Now they worked side-by-side in the training center.

I think Harry pulled a few strings to get Val as my tester. He was trying his best to make sure I got through this and knew Val might be a little easier going than some of the others. Not only that, he was leaving for Daytona Beach the next morning and said it was personally important to him that I pass this damn test.

Val and I walked out to the truck. This was it. Everything depended on me now. David, CDL stuffed in his wallet, out playing on the skid pad while I took this test, had fulfilled his half of the bargain. He was home free, and it was my turn to fly solo. If I botched these next couple of hours, I'd botch everything we'd planned.

It was the same truck I'd been in all week and I knew its idiosyncrasies – like how impossible it was to stick it in reverse. It took two hands to yank over the heavy spring-loaded gearshift. We started out with the pre-trip inspection, and I rattled off as many of the one-hundred-thirty-two things as I could. I think I impressed the hell out of Val. However, when she asked me in a quiet voice to talk about the fifth wheel, I realized I'd forgotten one of the single most critical areas of the truck – the entire coupling mechanism.

Val used a standardized score sheet listing all the skills that have to be demonstrated during the test. A sloppy or non-existent skill gets points off. Twenty-five points off is still passing, but twenty-six or more gets you a week of remedial driving practice and a final chance to re-take the test. Doing something exceptionally dangerous stops the test completely and sets you back a week, and the examiner drives you back to your classroom.

We climbed in the cab and did a pump down, checking the air compressor, the warning lights and buzzers, air leaks, brakes. I remembered everything. Val was busy ticking things off the sheet on her clipboard. I was feeling pretty smart.

"We're ready to drive," she said. "Exit the facility and turn left."

I'd done this every day for the past six or seven. There was a slight incline at the stop sign, and I knew enough not to roll back. I stood on the brake.

"I hope you don't mind if I talk to myself," I said to Val. "It's the only way I can drive."

I still had this habit of talking to myself non-stop, giving myself verbal instructions about what gear I was in, what gear came next. Even though he denied it, this talking drove A. G. crazy, but Harry ignored it. "Whatever works," he said.

"Okay with me," Val said, and I started talking to myself.

For the next half hour we drove through Green Bay, Val giving me left-turn, right-turn instructions to take us on the testing route. I announced beforehand exactly what I'd be doing every single step of the way. We drove on four-lane highways outside of town at top speed. We exited ramps and downshifted on the way to stop signs. We rolled into second gear flawlessly at stoplights. I was charmed.

It was time to head back to the training center. I recognized immediately the nasty hill where I'd have to make a bump and run in fourth to a left-hand turn. I'd never done it right and didn't do it right this time either. In the past I'd done it worse – actually came to a full stop and stalled the engine twice. This time I forgot to switch the range selector on the shift and was trying to make the slow turn in eighth, which doesn't work. Somehow, I got it back into neutral, selector switch down for low range, into fourth and made the turn without coming to a dead stop. Val ticked a few marks on her sheet.

We pulled into the facility.

"Set-up along the cones for a forty-five degree back," she said. I stopped and she got out of the truck.

This was the hardest part of the test, and my heart pounded. Parking was taught using a formula based on following the position of the hour hands on a clock. There was nothing intuitive about it, nothing that made any sense to me even still. I just followed the formula and hoped for the best. David later confessed to the same frustration until, one day, he finally got it. I wasn't remotely close to getting it. This wild card was likely to be a joker.

I rolled along in second gear past the cones, made an abrupt right-hand turn to the twelve o'clock position, straightened out for a split second, made an abrupt left-hand turn to the nine o'clock position, rolled six feet to straighten the steers, came to a stop, put on my four-way flashers, tooted twice, and struggled into reverse pulling the heavy shift toward me with both hands. Then I rolled straight back the prescribed fifteen feet, searched my left mirrors for the cones and the hole, saw Val watching me, started my lefter-looser turn to align the tractor with trailer, overdid it and immediately turned the whole maneuver into a blind-side back. I couldn't see anything. So I stopped, got into second gear, rolled forward to straighten out (not nearly far enough I learned later), and was face to face with another Schneider student practicing backing on the lot in front of the testing area. I couldn't move forward any further.

"Shit!" I said. "How the hell am I supposed to do this when he's in my way?" No one heard me spitting curses in the cab.

So I started backing again, unable to see anything except Val and her clipboard. And I pulled forward. And then backward. And forward. My arms were aching from the heavy gearshift spring. I knew there were only so many "pull-ups" before the test was canceled, and I knew that if you touched a cone, the test was canceled. My back left tandems, the side I could see, almost kissed the cones. Val came up to the truck and said, "Pull around to the straight backing cones." My forty-five backing test was canceled. I knew I'd just failed the test, had single-handedly blown our chances. At the most, I could look forward to a third week of remedial training, a last chance effort Schneider would make for us flunking students, with a third instructor. David would be long gone down the road with his training engineer.

But right now, I still had to go through the motions of finishing the test. I pulled through the straight backing lane and figured I should at least finish like a champ. Straight backing was easy for me. I straight backed through all the cones until I could see Val receding in the distance, waving at me to stop and come back.

She got in the truck, told me where to park, and we got out. This would be a great disappointment for Harry who was packed and ready for a cycle vacation to Daytona. And David would be distressed, visions of team driving all but evaporated.

"You passed," she said. "Sixteen points. Would have been fifteen if you'd remembered to toot on your straight back."

"How could I pass?" I argued. "I failed the forty-five."

"That's six points. And you did so well on the driving route, you had points to spare."

I didn't mention how she'd prompted me on the fifth wheel inspection. Why remind her?

Harry was visibly proud of me. A group of us were shuttled to the local DOT office to have our photos taken. I felt like Rocky, arms up, standing over his knock-out, with his heavyweight championship belt in his big, strong hand. For me, it was my laminated CDL in my little brown wallet.

7

This simplified our lives. If I hadn't passed, David would have been a week ahead, or two weeks, or three weeks, or whatever additional time it would have taken me to catch up. Eventually, either Schneider or I would have folded our cards, but now I'd passed, and we were both ready to take the next step.

We wouldn't be taking it together. The next step, called road training, involved two weeks of actual, over-the-road driving, pick-ups and deliveries with our private, individual training engineers delivering real loads to real customers.

We headed back to Madison and waited for the phone to ring. One day later I got my call. Justin Matherne was my training engineer. He was male.

When the Schneider form came around before our training engineers were assigned, David wondered aloud whether it had been a smart idea for me to check "no preference" on the training engineer's gender question. For me, personality was more critical than gender and so was teaming with a non-smoker. I'd known plenty of snippy women, fewer snippy men. I figured I'd keep my training engineer busy enough avoiding disasters. Finding a non-smoker from the pool of trainers would be a coup.

Over the phone, Justin described the sleeping arrangements in his tractor. Most Schneider cab-overs had one double bed in back. I hadn't considered this when I checked "no preference" on the gender question. His had double-decker bunks. What good news.

"How cold does it get?" I asked.

"Bring two sleeping bags, one stuffed inside the other," he said.

My sleeping bag, a goose down Frostline kit I'd made in a previous lifetime and was especially proud of, easily kept me warm in the dead of winter in an unheated metal vacation trailer we kept up north. I couldn't imagine being inside two of them.

"Thirty-five below in Minnesota last month," he said. "Pretty darn cold." He spoke like a gentleman.

"Well, if I take two, my husband won't have one." I put extra emphasis on *husband*.

"I understand you'll be teaming for Kimberly-Clark," Justin said. "I'm a Kimberly-Clark dedicated, so you'll see some Kimberly accounts. First load is to Sam's Club in Southfield, Michigan. Need to be there by Tuesday at twenty-two hundred."

Truckers use military time. So did my army father. But it had been many, many years since I had to tell when the commissary would open or the post pool would close in military time. Twenty-two hundred seemed pretty late on the civilian clock.

"So," Justin wound up, "I'll see you Monday at o-seven-hundred. And, by the way, there's no smoking in my truck."

That gave David and me a couple more days for last minute purchases. It was heaven to think about something other than getting that CDL, something like spending money in a mall. We needed sunglasses. Although we always wear sunglasses while driving, we'd never spent more than $8 a pair. We tend to pick them up when we see something that looks interesting or cheap. A quick search found sixteen pairs stashed around the house and car glove compartments. Most were broken or their plastic lenses scratched from sliding across the dash board. We visited a couple of shopping malls and got the pitch on price and features of real glass sunglasses with ultraviolet protection and polarized coatings.

We ended up at the Sunglass Hut in the middle of pedestrian traffic in a local mall. I didn't need a prescription lens, so I shopped the shelves and got hooked on a pair of Maui Jim top-of-the-line snazzy wire frames for $225 plus tax. Made in Japan, they featured every coating known to science, and there was a tricky polarized display that you could only read looking through the polarized Maui Jim's. David watched in amazement while the woman he'd known for eighteen years seriously considered spending $215 more than ever before on a pair of driving glasses. To my eyes it looked like the first tax-deductible expense in a $40,000 per year career. We left with the real glass Maui Jim's complete with neck cord and semi-hard carrying case and return receipt in the event there might be a change of heart. With our first paycheck still a month away, the cash flow was submarined into negative territory.

On the way home we made a pit-stop at Radio Shack. David still needed a few gizmos like a $50 power supply to run the computer from the cigarette lighter socket; a $20 hand-held two-way radio so one of us could wing-walk behind the truck when we backed into tight spaces in total darkness; a $5 splitter for plugging two or three things into one cigarette lighter socket; and a $90 electric refrigerator that plugs into the splitter, available at Wal-Mart.

So we wheeled into Wal-Mart and past the aisle to electric refrigerators when David spotted the optical department. His left eye needed a little more help than regular +2.00 magnifiers. For map reading in a car he was always switching between sunglasses and reading glasses and never could see the odometer wearing ordinary sunglasses. Bifocal sunglasses with shading on the top half seemed like the right choice. Wal-Mart had a $33 exam price, so we set up an appointment.

Next day, with his glasses prescription in hand, he faced the walls of frames. Frames come in four price ranges and each range had forty styles. Each style came with four optional coatings and bifocal features. That made six-hundred-forty possibilities. It kills me to watch him faced with this kind of decision. It takes forever. Finally, he chose line-less bifocals at considerable extra cost because he was convinced he looked younger. Then he chose the low-priced aviator gold wire frames in the gray tint instead of the five other colors. He chose the scratch proof coating on plastic lenses rather than glass because they were lighter and cost less. He chose the polarized coating, but since most people say that ultraviolet rays don't penetrate windshields, he passed on UV coating. At $145 they were about the cheapest line-less bifocal sunglasses he could get, eighty dollars less than mine, but still $135 more than he'd ever paid. He looked like a gangster in his, while for just an extra sixty dollars, I looked like an aging movie star.

After testing David's new lightweight plastic glasses, I started worrying about the weight of my Maui Jims, so we borrowed a letter scale from the customer service desk and weighed a bunch of typical glass and plastic glasses. Glass weighs from one to two ounces while plastic weighs a good half-ounce less. David's big plastic bifocals weighed about one ounce to Maui Jim's one and a half ounces. I decided to stick with Jim, but they weren't as perfect as they were the day before.

We still had one big, expensive project at home. David quizzed our next door neighbor, an airline pilot, about home security systems. Jim's trips kept him away three or four days every week so he had a security system in his house and a huge mailbox to handle postal pile-ups. David called Jim's security company and learned that systems typically consist of a control panel, a telephone dialing device, indoor and outdoor sirens, break-in detectors on windows and doors, motion detectors, fire detectors, high temperature and low temperature detectors. They range from $500 to $3000 depending on the number of detectors and electronic bells and whistles on the controller, plus $20 to $30 per month service fee. When the controller senses a problem, it sounds the alarm and dials the telephone to signal a control room at the service provider. The provider then follows up with checks to eliminate false alarms, then calls the police or fire department and your neighbor or relatives.

It wasn't our objective to be protected from intruders while we were fast asleep in the upstairs bedroom. We needed something that summoned help while we were exploring Pocatello. David opted for the basic system with two motion detectors to spot looters, two fire detectors, and a freeze detector. A little beeper inside tells if the system is set right, and an outside siren chases away thieves and attracts attention. It's something we probably needed for fifteen years, but never so urgently except for the time six years earlier when lightning struck the house while we were at work. That wrecked the fax machine and a couple of telephones and made a big black smudge on the wall where an electronic power supply transformer blew up. The ash tree that lightening hit starting dying immediately. David's guess was it would have killed a security alarm system, too.

Faced with another decision more costly and complicated than sunglasses, David decided to procrastinate on the security system to see if we flunked out of school or quit voluntarily. Instead, he did something we'd been talking about ever since we'd bought our video camera in Hong Kong ten years earlier – made a videotape of the contents of our house and put it in the safe deposit box. And waited for his training engineer to call.

It was time for me to go road training and leave David behind. He was looking forward to a couple of days at home, time to fight a nasty cold that kept him coughing for the last week. Not even pneumonia, however, would have kept him from driving me to Milwaukee to meet Justin, the man I'd be living with for two weeks. We arrived in Milwaukee Monday morning at o-seven-hundred. David checked out Justin and, satisfied, drove back to Madison and waited for his training engineer to call.

Justin Matherne had been a Red Lobster restaurant manager for twenty years. A year and a half before I met him, he was laid off. He was about forty-two, father of three, had shiny black hair and a non-standard trucker's body which means "no belly." It took him about ten minutes to review Schneider's expectations with me. The deal was I would drive 95% of the time. "Maybe 98%," he said. Further, he would be up front in the passenger seat the entire time, not sleeping. I liked that. Still talking my way through every maneuver, I needed him on alert ready to stop me before a repeat of the A. G. disaster.

He would teach me to use "Star Serve," the on-board computer and global positioning (GPS) system that tells Schneider where every truck in its fleet is at any moment. Unless you're in a tunnel, you cannot hide from Schneider. In return for this loss of privacy, a computer messaging system means quicker dispatches, instant directions to hundreds of locations, and instant answers to questions about a load. So, unlike many drivers without such a system, we wouldn't need to find a phone, call our dispatcher and get put on hold, wait for a return call at a phone booth, all which waste time and in the rain, get you wet. Our next load would be dispatched before our current one was delivered. Theoretically.

"And, we'll be going to Canada, so when you have free time, you should read the section about clearing customs."

I was encouraged about the notion of free time. A time manager like Justin must have devised plenty of ways to use time efficiently, to save time on the road and spend it instead with his wife and kids at home. A person with brains and the right skills could make this job work. I couldn't have hoped for a better training engineer.

Justin and I headed out for his tractor, a relatively new "condo" cab-over owned and operated by Kimberly-Clark until Schneider took over their account a year and a half ago. It was a white tractor, not the typical pumpkin orange Schneider tractor. It looked a little like a bald-faced hornet, square-headed with big compound windshield eyes. Tractor number "30369." Stuck on the driver's window was a decal of a girl lizard standing on its hind legs with a circle and slash through it, the universal "do not enter" symbol for "lot lizards" or, more to the point, truck stop whores.

Justin's truck was a nine-speed. What a break. Almost every tractor in the Schneider fleet was a ten-speed. I'd heard random conversations up in Green Bay that we'd all be driving ten-speeds after graduation. No one except me seemed to think it was a big deal. A ten-speed, I groaned – after memorizing, practicing, burning the gearshift pattern of a nine speed into my itty-bitty brain. Sixth gear on a ten-speed was where first gear on a nine-speed is and seventh is where sixth was, and on and on. Just something more to fan my anxiety.

But, number 30369 was a nine-speed with every gear just where it should be. One thing different was the front steer axle location – it was set either farther back or farther forward, I was never sure which. Whatever it was, it didn't matter to me. I'd either be able to make the turn or not depending on how well I managed the space. I was too new to realize how much every inch of wheelbase affected a truck's turning radius.

Inside, however, this tractor was totally different from any cab-over I'd seen. By hunching over like a short, three-foot tall person, you ducked through a passageway between the front seats and stood upright in the very tall airspace behind the seats. This is what made Justin's cab-over a "condo."

On either side outboard of the transmission hump behind the seats, there were deep pits. If you should mismanage your step one way or the other, you'd sink to your knees into a well behind the seats. The wells were usually filled with pillows and sleeping equipment from the upper bunk which tumbled down in transit. "Rides like a truck" means that nothing stays put if it's not tied down.

The bottom bunk was safe. The top bunk was not safe. The top bunk was shoulder level above the transmission hump. That meant you had to use Justin's portable Coleman refrigerator to stand on in order to throw your leg up into the bunk and then pull the rest of your body in after it. I wasn't to practice this until it was time for bed, but I queried Justin anyway about the safety of this lofty sleeping perch. The shelf was only about twenty-nine inches wide, without rails, and my sleeping bag spilled over the edge.

"Many of your students end up on the floor?" I asked.

"Not many," he said.

I stowed my duffel bag, my extra tennis shoes, my warm weather clothes in case we went south, my briefcase with my Schneider Reference Guide and Trip Planning book, and my atlas in a second loft above the passenger seat. It was capacious. I could have brought more, but I was learning to restrain myself.

When I finished, Justin was seated in the passenger's seat. This was it. I'd be driving. It had been three days since I'd last shifted anything other than the syncro-meshed Dodge Colt Vista, and I hoped it would all come back to me.

"Don't forget," Justin said, "you have a fifty-three foot trailer behind you, not forty-eight."

This would be another first. The instructors at Green Bay casually mentioned the fifty-three-foot trailer as the length we'd usually pull, but they never gave us one to pull through their hometown.

Not in a hurry to reveal my unique shifting style, I tried dawdling. I adjusted my air-ride seat by fiddling with each of the six adjustments – height, downward or upward tilt on the front of the seat cushion, forward or backward distance from the steering wheel, angle of tilt for the seat back, more or less lumbar support, and finally whether to oscillate or lock the action of the seat.

Oscillation of the seat helps reduce back slap. Imagine the tractor as a pyramid with the driver at the top point, steer wheels at the front and drive wheels at the back. When the front wheels go over a bump it causes the top of the pyramid (driver) to rock back and forth as well as up and down. When the back wheels go over the bump, the top of the pyramid lurches forward and back. This is more pronounced in tractors with a short wheelbase and tall cabs. Cab-over tractors are the worst; big, long conventionals are not as bad. The oscillating seat floats on short horizontal slides while the cab oscillates. It's recommended for people eager to retire with a functioning neck. I'd never used the oscillation feature because when you do, your seat moves back as you depress the clutch. Coordinating the shift lever, clutch and throttle pedals for smooth shifting had been hard enough without a fourth dimension. I decided to keep the seat fixed and oscillate on top of it rather than with it. By the end of the day, I'd changed my mind.

In second gear, which I found without help, I eased out of the parking spot between two other fifty-three footers, watching in the convex mirror as I turned tentatively a little to the right aiming toward the exit. The end of the 53' trailer was nowhere to be seen. Everything in a convex spot mirror is distorted, naturally, and almost impossible for the rookie brain to de-scramble on short notice. I shouldn't have worried because Justin was fixed like an eagle on his mirror and coached me the whole way. "Okay, your tandems are past his steers. Turn now. Now. Now. NOW!"

I turned, still aiming for the exit that was barred by a lift-gate. It takes forever for a long trailer to finally line up behind the tractor, but when it did, I shifted into third with a nasty grind. Justin, very patiently, said, "Every tractor takes getting used to." I loved this man.

We stopped at the gate, checked out with Schneider on the intercom, and we were on our way down I-94 to Michigan via Chicago.

It was beginning to snow. Justin turned on the radio and tuned in one of Chicago's all-news stations for a traffic and weather report. I was concentrating on merging traffic.

"Bummer," he said. "Lake effect snow on I-94. Let's take the Tri-State."

Part of my assignment before meeting Justin was to prepare a trip plan that would get us from Milwaukee to Southfield the quickest, shortest, cheapest way. By using the atlas and the Trip Planning Guide, I'd determined the best route to Southfield was via I-94, US 41, I-90 and I-69 into Detroit. I had it all written down and in my mind. No Tri-State. Plus the Tri-State had many toll-gates and added a few miles to the trip. I really thought my way was better.

"Take the Tri-State," Justin said as I equivocated. "You'll be glad you did."

I wasn't convinced. It took five hours to get to Gary, Indiana, via the Tri-State. My way took three. My way had no toll roads. His had many toll booths. That meant changing lanes, stopping, starting, shifting. Both ways were snowy, slippery, and for an inaugural run, absolute murder. But what did I know. Looking back on it, bigger warnings should have been going off in my head – my first road trip was taking me through Chicago in rush hour. What insanity!

For starters, tractor 30369's driver's side windshield washer did not work. It piddled a sick, little dribble of solvent in a five-inch arc at the bottom of the windshield and smeared salt and road grime over the balance. I hunched as low as I could to peer over the steering wheel and out the clean spot, even lowered my air-ride seat, but couldn't see squat.

Secondly, it was morning rush hour in Chicago and while this particularly affects inbound commuters, it's murder on truck traffic on the Tri-State bypass. Trucks, it turns out, are as plentiful outbound and cross town as they are inbound. There were lines of salt-crusted trucks and cars inching along through six inches of dirty, black snow and ice, stacking up at the tollbooths. They weren't rookies like me. They knew whether to be in the right lane or middle lane, which lane would become an "exit only" lane, which toll booth lane to inch toward, and if it weren't for Justin's coaching, I would still be in Chicago. Consider choosing a lane with mostly big trucks, he'd say, since it just takes a few toll-paying trucks to quickly make a long line shrink.

Lake Michigan is a natural barrier. All east-west traffic north of Indianapolis has to pass around the southern tip of the lake. Half a dozen interstates feed in from the west; Interstates 65, 80, 90, and 94 all feed in from the east. But around the tip of the lake they all merge into I-80 which is possibly the most overloaded fifteen miles of road in America.

"I've never seen it this bad," he said. I believed him because at one point he said matter-of-factly, "Better take my blood pressure pills," and he popped two.

When at last we were within reach of the Schneider Operating Center in Gary, Indiana, we were so late that the on-time delivery to Southfield, Michigan, was out of the question. We couldn't possibly make it with the legal driving hours I had left since they'd been used up in the stop and go traffic.

"Bummer," Justin said. "We have to find a relay."

This was one of the big advantages of having such a sophisticated communication system operating right from the tractor. Soon after Justin realized we couldn't make the delivery and sent that message to headquarters, Schneider found someone nearby who could finish the run. He was actually waiting for us at the entrance to the Gary yard. He followed us in his bobtail, we uncoupled, he coupled up and left. It took ten minutes. I was happy to see our load go out the gate.

I parked the bobtail in soupy mud as close to the door of the OC as I could, which this night was about a quarter of a mile away. Ruts and ankle deep slop lay between us and dinner. I fished my clunky, rubber-soled boots out of the deep well behind Justin's seat.

Schneider OC's are company-owned and operated facilities located, at that time, in eleven different locations across the country (one in Canada). They're all laid out similarly with a large dining area, a cafeteria or a grill, a television lounge with huge movie selection, free laundry, and above all, individual, meticulously cleaned shower rooms with thick towels, soap, benches, toilet, sink, etc. A complete maintenance shop fixes tractors and trailers round-the-clock, and several fuel islands pump Schneider's personal stock of bulk diesel fuel. Some have a drive-through truck wash; all have vacuums and stalls for easy cab cleaning. Drivers are encouraged to fill up here rather than on the road, and trip planning always includes timely fuel stops.

The Gary OC was a busy place that night. West-bounders had bailed out before heading into the snow we'd just slogged through. East-bounders like us were bailing because of the exhausting conditions we'd just left. It was gratifying to hear these professionals bitch about weather back in Chicago.

It was the first real look at my fellow Schneider drivers, most of whom were not trainees like me, but judging from the "years of service" patches on their sleeves, veteran drivers. Most wore some sort of clothing to identify them with the company. Justin had a full uniform: black jacket with orange Schneider insignia, gray pin-striped shirt with orange Schneider embroidery, black pants, rubber slip-on shoes, a Schneider hat. There was no mistaking him for anything but a Schneider driver.

But others clearly weren't following the unwritten Schneider dress code which proscribed key chains, leathers, and cowboy boots. They had them all. They wore tattoos, leather vests, earrings, Harley T-shirts, rock group T-shirts, metal-toed cowboy boots, faded jeans, overalls. There were more skin colors than dolls come in, more hair-dos than in a magazine – long, lovely ponytails I would have died for, short ones like David's, curly gray ones, ponytails on balding men, one bona fide ducktail.

There were women in tight Schneider outfits, women like me in jeans and sweaters, others in overalls. I recognized a gorgeous black woman who'd been on the Schneider recruitment video tape sitting at a table right across from me. She was dressed to the nines in Schneider black and orange. Her hair was slicked back in a twist, and her dimples were deep. Men were staring with good reason. It would have been good to get her autograph before she's discovered.

There was an Amazonian woman behind the counter who'd overdosed on steroids and protein. A short-haired lesbian couple ate quietly in the midst of trucker chatter, their Schneider jackets slung side-by-side over chair backs.

Nobody, however, wore a feathered urban cowboy hat or oversized belt buckle. Somehow, Schneider had been able to enforce that part of the dress code on this independent, disparate group of men and women. Not that the cowboy look wasn't represented – the boots and a dozen jangling keys latched to a belt loop defined the fashion-forward Western statement.

Still, it was nothing like we'd see in the next two weeks – the real cowboys of the road who worked long and hard on their frontier images, spending paychecks on tooled boots, Texas belt buckles, bells and whistles. Justin and I once lingered by a rig standing proud at an Illinois rest area, lit like a Christmas tree and decorated in fancy script that spelled "Lamar and Judy Ann Schmidke" above the name of their truck, "Always Loaded." Wish we could have waited long enough for Lamar and Judy Ann to return in their matching outfits.

The closest Schneider got to that was with some owner-operators who had paid for their own tractors and, by golly, were going to put on as much chrome and as many lights as they damn well could. I started keeping a record of exactly how many lights can fit on a tractor-trailer combination. It's somewhere north of 100.

Justin and I worked our way through the cafeteria line. In front of me, a driver's mashed potatoes and gravy slid off one edge onto the plastic tray, his four pieces of fried chicken towered high above his double dinner rolls. His Stop-N-Go coffee mug was the nine-incher.

Justin made a point earlier saying we'd only eat one hot meal a day and the rest would come from the cooler. This sounded like a warning and since all I had in the cooler was yogurt and string cheese, I soon had more cafeteria food on my plate than I'd ever eaten in my life. Boiled new potatoes rolling around in butter and parsley, meatloaf, green beans, corn, coleslaw, dinner rolls. This was not the stay thin plan. And I knew it wasn't good to eat this much late at night. But I was starving and welcomed an excuse to stay in the cafeteria and eavesdrop on the war stories.

The men at my table, east-bounders, were telling about a flatbed back on the Tri-State that lost its load of 15,000 pound steel coils, right in the middle of the highway. The chain binders and chain assembly broke and the three huge coils rolled onto the pavement. Traffic backed up for ten miles waiting for heavy equipment to move the debris. We'd heard about it on the CB. Since the flatbed was a west-bounder, it hadn't affected our trip at all, but those poor folks going west – it must have taken them an extra three hours to get through Chicago. Weather-related stories were flying back and forth across the table. Drivers ate their dinners with one eye glued to the 24-hour weather channel on the television overhead.

Once that flatbed story was finished, other flatbed stories followed. Stories about flipped flatbeds, de-coupled flatbeds, flatbeds rear-ending passenger cars, whole families being wiped out by driving under flatbeds they couldn't see on dark, rainy nights. Then came the van stories about vans hitting bridges and toll booths and low-clearance overpasses. Then came the wiggle-wagon stories about wiggle-wagons fish-tailing in high winds and flipping. And then the hazardous materials stories. I got weary.

I found a telephone and called David. He was sick in bed, still waiting for a call from his training engineer.

"You having fun?" he asked.

It was a hard question to answer because, no, I was not having fun. But I knew that's not what he wanted to hear. I knew he was so eager for this new life to work out and so worried it wouldn't. He'd seen what a struggle Green Bay had been for me; he knew just how little was intuitive; he was discouraged about not starting his road training on time.

"I got lots of shifting practice going through Chicago," I said cheerfully. "And I did all the driving."

"Good, that's great!" he urged.

"And the food here's not bad." I added. "And Justin's a good guy."

"Patient?"

"Very."

I paused. "But I'm not sure how fun it is yet."

I have a hard time lying.

Back at the tractor, Justin was sending another message to headquarters telling them the relay had taken place, that we were ready for another load. He was running the engine to warm up the cab on this bitterly cold night and to keep the fuel from jelling. So was everyone else – probably one hundred tractors bedding down in this location, all roaring, all belching. Schneider drivers' monthly bonuses are tied to idling time. Overnight idling will cost a driver part of his bonus because it wastes fuel and is actually harder on the engine than shutting down and restarting in the morning. Only below 10 degrees was overnight idling authorized.

Schneider engine computers were set up to shut off the engine if it idled more than a few minutes. To keep it idling longer, the cruise control had a function that would keep the engine idling at 1000 rpm. Schneider decided that was the best speed for reconciling good engine lubrication with low fuel consumption.

As rookies, we'd never heard about any other company having the "no idling" policy. Driving past smoggy rest areas and truck stops leads you to believe all trucks always idle. With two billion dollars to spend on his company every year, Don Schneider certainly should have been able to do the research and formulate the most profitable policy. He must have concluded that long idling is hard on an engine and on fuel consumption. The flip side to having a policy like that was the possibility that other companies placed a higher priority on keeping drivers happy. Drivers waking up to start the day in an 11-degree bedroom may not start the day happy about their employer.

It was cold enough that night for all the owner/operators to keep cozy in their rumbling cabs, but not cold enough to get below 10 degrees. Justin switched off the engine.

Time for me to re-position my sleeping bag and pillow, climb up on the sleeping ledge and finally fall gratefully asleep. Justin stayed up front while I closed the curtains between the passenger area and the sleeping compartment, hoisted myself up and burrowed, fully clothed, into my sleeping bag.

"Thanks," I said, and he switched off the light and climbed into the lower bunk.

8

Next to us in this yard was a "reefer," a refrigerated trailer with an engine-driven compressor running on automatic. It runs along at a low speed for about a half-hour and then, with a roar, cranks into high speed for fifteen minutes keeping its perishable contents either warm or cold. Part of truck driving is being able to sleep along side these snoring giants.

Shortly after the reefer switched into its minor mode, I heard the beeper of our Star Serve satellite go off. It beeped and beeped again.

"Justin," I whispered. "Are you awake?"

"Of course," he said. "Can't sleep beside a reefer."

"The computer's beeping."

"Bummer." Justin regularly responded with 'bummer' whether news was good or bad.

"Do you want me to climb down and read it?" I knew this was a dumb offer because it was pitch black and I'd kill myself.

"No," he said. "I'll get it."

He opened the curtains into the bright greenish mercury vapor lights of the yard, read the message and said, "Back through Chicago tomorrow, pick up an empty in Waukegan, shuttle to Baxter Health Care, wait for our next load."

"What time tomorrow?" I asked.

"We should be out of here by o-four-hundred. If you want a shower, up at o-three-hundred."

Three in the morning, that is. It was about ten at night now.

"If you want breakfast, earlier than that. I'll set the clock for o-two-thirty. That early enough for you?"

"Okay," I said.

I don't normally fall asleep knowing I have to wake up a few hours later. I've never been able to fall asleep before a big trip. On a business trip, getting up for a 6:30 AM departure at the airport meant I didn't fall asleep until I was on the plane.

But this was the exception that may have been the first sign of success as a truck driver. In spite of the roaring reefer next to us cycling on and off, I fell asleep. Justin didn't snore, not that I could have heard him. It was pitch black behind the curtains of the cab, freezing cold on my cheeks which I remedied with a blanket draped over my head. Dead tired, I slept until Justin's clock buzzed at 02:30.

Like a slow-motion nymph, I emerged from the sleeping bag, slid down the bunk onto the portable refrigerator, lifted my duffel from the loft, opened the curtains, turned off the alarm, closed the curtains, sat in the driver's seat, threaded my arms under the steering wheel, laced up my boots while wishing for slip-on's like Justin's, took my keys from the ignition, found the recessed door handle, opened it, moved onto the threshold four and half feet above the ground, stood up outside holding onto the steering wheel, pulled the duffel onto the seat I'd just vacated, grabbed the handholds outside the door, felt for the other two steps to the ground which was, by now, frozen, rutted mud, reached up for my duffel, slid it onto my shoulder, closed the door quietly and trekked to the operating center for a shower.

There was plenty of activity in the lot when I emerged from my sleeping bag cocoon. I'd entered a 24/7 blue-collar world. Trucks were moving around, drivers doing pre-trips, fueling, lights were on in maintenance where a pneumatic impact wrench fired like a machine gun, hammering lug nuts onto trailer wheels. But inside, there was no waiting line for showers. An attendant behind the service counter assigned me shower room #121. Inside, I put the duffel on a bench, laid out a cosmetics case, hair dryer, flip flops (David, with boot camp experience, insisted I buy these although my feet had never known athlete's foot), clean underwear, clean socks, clean turtleneck. I planned to wear my dirty jeans which, I could see in the bright light of the bathroom, had long, black schmisses of grease from the fifth wheel. I stirred a tablespoon of Citrucel into cold water as a constipation antidote which, incidentally, does not work.

Schneider spares neither hot water nor towels for its drivers. I washed my short hair twice, stood under the showerhead for fifteen minutes, and took all the time in the world for this luxury. I fluffed my hair a little, put make-up over a couple of persistent age spots, laced up my hateful boots, and returned the key.

Justin was eating breakfast in the dining area. Assuming this was going to be the single hot meal of the day, I loaded up on corned beef hash, potatoes and eggs.

"How'd you sleep?" he asked.

"Better than I thought possible. And you?"

"Never should park next to a reefer."

After breakfast, I called home. A message from David said he was headed to Milwaukee to train with a driver who had a regular, hazardous materials run back and forth from Milwaukee to Chicago. He'd be working with him until someone running the nationwide system was available. Hazardous didn't have much appeal for me. Neither did Chicago. I wondered how David felt about it.

Meanwhile, Justin and I were getting to know each other pretty well. I'd never been in a situation, except for school in Green Bay, where my inadequacies were so humiliatingly exposed. There was no hiding missed gears or misjudged corners. Turn signals, which are not self-canceling on a truck, would blink on for miles before I'd notice. At toll booths, I'd roll just past the outstretched hand of the collector, ten inches beyond where I could conveniently reach it, so I'd have to open the door, lean out backward, and pay my dollar and a quarter.

Justin saw it all. He must have been an excellent manager during his Red Lobster days, and he knew exactly how to handle me. He was so patient, so forgiving, so understanding, so honest. It was clear why Schneider paid these guys extra to train us. At one point I asked him why on earth he was driving a truck and not looking for a management position in the Schneider hierarchy.

"Actually, I'm trying to sell my house and move to Green Bay. Once I do that, I think there'll be a management job for me. Schneider won't consider me until I move," he answered.

Then he asked a poignant question. "What do your kids think of their mother being a truck driver?"

I could only guess at what my kids really thought. Truck driving wasn't hypothetical now, wasn't just another of their mother's amusing diversions. Mother was a truck driver. Their father, an internationally prominent pediatrician who specialized in medical ethics, was the kind of parent a kid could be proud of. *The New York Times* quoted him periodically about things that mattered. He served at the time on the Board of Trustees of Princeton University, his alma mater. He was personal friends with Eunice Shriver.

So when my kids talked about their parents, did they brag about Norman or did they brag about me?

I begged the question.

But Justin, father of three, was concerned enough about what his kids' classmates thought that he was ready to get back into management. Too bad, I thought. Too bad kids are as judgmental now as they've always been. I recounted a military incident that happened to me in the fifth grade. We'd just moved to Sault Ste. Marie, Michigan, where my father was assigned to help operate the Soo Locks during the Korean War. In a perpetual effort to make new friends in new schools, I'd had previous success bragging about my father's military experience. This time, I tried to impress a few little girls by inviting them to explore my dad's army trunks still unpacked in the attic. We dug down and found his cross country track medals from Penn State and then, in a special hinged box, his Purple Heart from World War II. I opened it for them, but when they begged to pin it on, I snapped the lid shut. Next day at school, during art class, six of my new "friends" drew big purple hearts with arrows through them, like silly cupid's hearts, which were not meant to be funny. It was a blow to my fifth grade ego. I went home crying.

Justin had stories like that. His father was a bomber pilot in the Air Force who retired as a lieutenant colonel. Mine was in the Corps of Engineers and retired as a lieutenant colonel. Justin lived everywhere, even Germany. I'd lived all over the United States, but when my parents were assigned to Afghanistan, I thought it would be more fun to stay by the side of my college boyfriend in East Lansing, a poor decision in hindsight.

For two weeks, we traded stories. Maybe it was designed to keep him awake. When it was time to make some critical commentary about one of my driving maneuvers, he'd just interrupt and do it. Stories never interfered with learning. He was paid to teach everything students needed to know before being let loose, in pairs, to an orange pumpkin truck of their own. That "au pair" driving which David and I would do together is called "C-teaming" and continues for four weeks after road training. After C-teaming, there's an automatic promotion to regular pay rate. For drivers planning to drive solo, C-teaming is their only chance to learn the ropes with another rookie in the truck to help figure everything out. And if a student is accident-free for six months, the trainer – Justin in this case – gets a bonus.

He taught me how to keep a legal log. Truck drivers are required by law to keep a daily log which shows in a graphical way how they spend every hour of a twenty-four hour day. Once you're a truck driver, you keep this log even on the days you're not driving. I'd heard a lot about drivers keeping two logs, much like Mafia accountants keep two sets of books.

Justin did not advocate any tinkering with logbooks. He abided by the fine print of the federal regulations and taught me to do it the same way. Justin may be the only man in the world who keeps a strictly legal logbook. David's training engineer, I learned later, said it was absolutely impossible to keep a legal logbook. Although with a recent change in logging rules, what he taught David back then was as far from federal law as you could get and was the more typical way experienced drivers kept logs. By logging less driving time and more time sleeping and by being clever enough not to be caught doing it at a weigh station, drivers, who are paid by the mile, can drive longer hours, more miles, and make more money. It's called unauthorized overtime in other professions.

Nevertheless, in Justin's world, whenever there was a "change of duty" among the four kinds of duty status – driving, sleeping, on duty, off duty – we logged the time of day to within a seven-and-a-half minute period, the geographic location to within the nearest tenth of a mile, the serial number of the trailer we were pulling, and the nature of the inspection we were performing – pre-trip, post-trip, or enroute.

Not only did we log an inspection, we did it. We made sure no one had pulled the pin on the fifth wheel which is a little trick kids in big cities like to play. They hide nearby and watch the tractor pull away while the trailer goes nowhere. We made sure the air lines to the brakes weren't cut, another little trick vandals pull. We thumped all eighteen tires listening for flats. Second time we did that, we found one and spent an unpaid hour having it fixed. We'd check each of the twenty lights. We'd check fuel, oil, anti-freeze levels just as you would in a car. We'd make sure the cab shell was hooked to the frame of the tractor so it wouldn't bounce up and open while you were speeding down I-94. We made sure the mirrors, all six of them, were adjusted properly.

During two weeks with Justin, we delivered tissues from Kimberly-Clark in Wisconsin to Sam's Club in Michigan, plastic pellets from Dow Chemical in Michigan to Kimberly-Clark in Wisconsin to melt into diaper liners, scrap paper from Jefferson Smurfit in Illinois for relay to Kimberly Clark in Connecticut, diapers and tampons from Wisconsin to Michigan, more plastic pellets for diaper liners back to Wisconsin, tissues to Sam's Club in Des Moines, Iowa, and special blue wooden pallets called Chep pallets from Webster City, Iowa, to Wisconsin.

That load of tissues in Iowa nearly wrecked my truck driving career. It had been an uneventful trip from Neenah, Wisconsin, through my hometown of Madison, on skinny, scenic US-151 through the familiar countryside of southwestern Wisconsin and into the twilight near Dubuque. We pulled into the Schneider facility at Des Moines just in time for a late dinner, our hot meal of the day, my shower deferred until morning.

Bright and early March 14, I showered, wolfed a hot breakfast, returned to the truck refreshed and did a thorough pre-trip inspection. Justin was ready in the passenger seat for a short drive to Sam's Club to make our delivery. I could never have been more alert.

Imagine my surprise as I pulled away from the parking place between the other two sleeping Schneider trucks, shifted carefully into third gear without grinding so as not to disturb the sleeping drivers in the adjacent trucks, pulled a little left button-hook to setup for a sharp right hand turn out the gate, and noticed my back left tandems finishing a trip over a trick guard rail. I say trick because I'm sure it wasn't there when I pulled out. I didn't feel a thing. All I heard was a gentle crushing sound, like a football fan squeezing an empty beer can, and it was over before I knew it.

I could have rolled on because Justin, busy anticipating the sharp right turn I needed to make, missed it all. The sleeping drivers hadn't flown open their curtains, jumped out of their trucks and flagged me down. The little smooshing sound of the twenty-foot galvanized guard rail breaking off its eight-by-eight wooden piers couldn't possibly have been heard by anyone but me. I could have ignored this tiny event.

But I'm far too honest. I seldom cheat. I never steal. With rare exception, I always tell the truth. Which really bugs David, who sneaks into a second movie at the multiplex without a pang.

"Justin," I said, "I've demolished the guard rail."

"Bummer."

"No, I mean it."

"I know you do. Pull around."

I re-parked between the sleeping pumpkins. We got out and examined the truck first. The metal rim of the left rear tandem showed a slight burr, nothing to report. The guardrail, however, was demolished. Snapped that sucker right off the pilings at ground level.

"I didn't feel a thing," I said.

"Imagine how it feels when you roll over a Honda. You can't feel that either. That's a real bummer."

"I'm finished. That's it. I'm retiring. It was a brief career, but I'm unsafe behind the wheel." I knew that with 12,000 drivers to choose from, Schneider sure didn't need one with an accident record in her first week of driving. An accident on their own property, no less. And so there I was again, responsible for ruining David's and my plans. We'd have to start from scratch, thinking up some way to earn a living, some way to spend our pre-retirement years. I'd figure out a way to call David from the OC and break the news.

"Let's go in and file a report," Justin said in a sympathetic, managerial voice, mindful of my despair.

Inside at the fuel desk, we were met by a churlish little man who yelped when I announced what I'd done. Even the woman who was assisting him was startled by his response.

"Not again!" he yelled. "Goddamn! So early in the morning. Why does this always happen to me?" I was wondering the same. And I'm sure Justin was secretly pissed over losing a bonus for having an accident-free student. What we learned at the fuel desk is that the trick guard rail had moved many times into the path of Schneider trucks. This made me feel better.

I decided it might be premature to retire at this point so, after reporting the accident by phone to insurance officials at Schneider, after having the guard rail photographed, after admitting to the head trainer at Schneider that yes, indeed, this accident could have been prevented, after being told I could appeal this blotch on my driving record if I felt there was reason to dispute it, I decided to mount the horse and ride again.

Meanwhile, by the time my two weeks of training with Justin had finished, David had been with his trainer for only one. For the first two days he'd been making pick-ups around Bedford Park near the Chicago Sanitary and Ship Canal on Chicago's south side, not very far from where his father grew up at 79th and Halsted. Typically, there were three stops at different warehouses in the toxic sinkholes of Chicago's industrial underbelly where they'd load a few dozen fifty-five gallon barrels and some palletized bags of powdered dry acid. They'd run it up to South Milwaukee and drop the trailer at a PPG (Pittsburgh Plate Glass) dock.

This was strictly a day job. Driving a day cab without sleeper or satellite communications but with a rear window, David's trainer, Kevin, made all his deliveries between 7:00 AM and 5:00 PM every weekday and spent every night and weekends at home. That meant David got to stay in a Milwaukee motel a few more nights, but he wasn't getting critical over-the-road experience.

What he was getting instead was great practice docking at crappy truck docks. Getting into one at a chemical company required blocking both eastbound lanes of a boulevard and doing a blind-side back into the long, narrow driveway between brick walls. Another was at the end of a very dark canopied tunnel so there was no way to see what you were backing into or over. There, you had to walk back, shade your eyes and give the area a good visual before backing into it. Even in excellent lighting, the mirrors can only show the edges of a backup zone. On a straight back, there are no mirrors to show what's passing under the trailer's DOT bumper. You have to know there's nothing back there before you start backing. Good luck.

After only two weeks of school, David was not quite up to this level in the backing department. Kevin stood outside by the driver's door and called the shots, "Clockwise, counterclockwise, tighter, looser, stop, pull-up."

But he was learning other things. He learned firsthand how hazardous material (hazmat) book learning differs from hazmat practice. In Green Bay we learned that critical hazmat shipping papers must be kept in the driver's door pouch so they'd be easy to reach in case of a spill or accident. But Kevin's method was to put the papers on the dashboard in the middle of the windshield where they were easy to see from the outside, not necessarily easy to reach. We also learned in school that hazmat laws required us to stop and check the tires every one hundred miles or two hours, whichever came sooner, to make sure they weren't hot enough to burst into flames. David didn't see a tire checked in two days. Kevin did, however, stop his conspicuously placarded truck before crossing railroad tracks.

On the third day, David hooked up with Ed, his official road engineer. Like Justin, "Fast Eddie" had an interesting work history. He was a Viet Nam vet with scars to prove it. Then he was a narcotics detective in Milwaukee with a souvenir bullet hole in his back, and now, for the past eleven years, a Schneider truck driver. There wasn't a subject he couldn't handle from economics to politics. His personal story reflected the challenges of being a black man, and the O. J. Simpson trial going on at the time fueled their conversation for hours.

By his own admission, Ed could stand to lose fifty pounds. Yet the supply of Ultra Slim Fast milk shakes stayed mostly untouched while he filled up on truck stop food at every opportunity, downing super-sized portions of deep-fat fried anything covered with salty gravy. Various chips and Ho-Ho's littered the engine cover, never out of arm's reach. One good snacking habit, sunflower seeds, saved him from runaway obesity. He got big bags of roasted, salted, unshelled sunflower seeds and for mile after mile his right arm would automatically reach out for a single seed, deliver it to his lips, receive the shell, drop the shell in the shell bag, and reach for another seed. With each seed taking a minute's time, a couple of hundred seeds kept him off the really bad food for over three hours.

Their first load originated at the Baxter Health Care warehouse in Waukegan, IL. Like Kimberly-Clark was to be our dedicated account, Baxter was Ed's. Having been there dozens of times, he knew the layout well, went to the right warehouse door to pick up the paper work, coupled up to the waiting trailer, checked the neat stacks of corrugated cartons containing hospital supplies and confirmed the door seal serial number.

Their destination was another Baxter warehouse in Montgomery, New York. Although there is a very straight and fast toll road, Interstate 80, which crosses Indiana and Ohio, Baxter didn't authorize paying the extra tolls. So Schneider drivers and other major haulers use slower state highway routes. Ed took the first demonstration shift through Chicago rush hour, calling David's attention to the right lane on I-94 that must be avoided if you don't intend to cross the Skyway, pointing out the express lanes that will get a trucker arrested, and the lane changes just to stay on I-94 at the I-55 interchange. Somewhere in Indiana on US Highway 6, within a stone's throw of the speedy toll road, Ed gave David his first turn to drive in the country on a road that followed county section lines and made sharp turns through small towns without by-passes.

In western Pennsylvania Ed took over again and drove into the night. Finally, after three weeks in the industry, David got his first real taste of team driving and spent his first night in a sleeper berth while Ed stretched his driving day past the fifteen hour limit. Eventually, even eleven year veterans have to sleep, and after midnight in a truck stop in eastern Pennsylvania, Fast Eddie parked the rig, leaned over to the right and fell asleep on the engine cover between the Ho-Ho's and potato chips. This would be the pattern throughout the week, Ed sleeping on the engine cover leaving David the whole queen sized bunk to himself. After delivering in Montgomery, they turned around and headed right back to Waukegan with a load of bedpans. This is what it was like to have a dedicated account.

It took David a few trips to learn the necessary tricks, but eventually he discovered how to get quality sleep in a moving truck. Ed's tractor was a cab-over with a wonderful big soft mattress, but at first it was like trying to fall asleep with a Green Bay Packer lineman at each corner shaking the mattress up, down, forward, backward, left, right. Trucks ride like a truck. If your ear is brushing against a blanket, pillow, shirt collar, or anything, you hear every scrape. And it's hard to sleep with your head flopping all over the place. His solution, and one we both eventually adopted, was to use a horseshoe-shaped pillow we bought in a truck stop. Wedged under your neck, a good horseshoe pillow allows your head to rock ever so slightly, like a baby in a cradle.

Truck noise takes getting used to. It's much louder than a regular vehicle's and has many variations. Up-shifting, down-shifting, stopping, starting, air horns, air brakes, CB talk, supplies rattling in the closets all add up to "noisy." Some of this can be minimized by driver technique and by careful stowing of gear. Using good quality earplugs in the sleeper berth eliminates most of it. Some is "white noise" and actually helps you fall asleep.

On the return trip through Pennsylvania's steep, scenic hills, David had his first opportunity to appreciate the wonders of cruise control and the engine jake brake installed on Schneider's International Navistar trucks. Mechanics had it set up so that when cruise control is on maximum, it keeps you rolling (in those days) at 56 mph (one mile an hour above Schneider's speed limit) on level ground or gentle hills. Plus, the engine control module gives you an extra thirty horsepower that's only available if cruise is engaged. On steep upgrades, you watch the speed fall off until a downshift is necessary, then double-clutch down to the next lower gear. Cruise control stays on throughout and applies full horsepower immediately to the lower gear, attempting to recapture 56 mph.

On downgrades, cruise control allows overspeed of 2 mph before it automatically applies the jake. A jake brake switches the intake and exhaust valve timing to utilize engine compression which slows the truck much more than ordinary backing off the throttle. At 2 mph overspeed, two cylinders are switched, at 3 mph overspeed four cylinders are switched, and at 4 mph overspeed, all six cylinders brake the engine and slow down the truck's race to the bottom. It makes the loud rapping, roaring, staccato sound with which we are all familiar. As long as speeds above 55 mph are being logged on the truck's computer with no throttle from the foot pedal, it doesn't count against the driver as speeding. Schneider tracked every second of overspeed and, if it exceeded 1% of total time driven, you'd lose your quarterly bonus.

Cruise control is a serious money-maker for drivers being paid by the mile. Without cruise, and with a pay deduction for overspeeding, you need to keep your speed under the limit to allow for the inevitable fluctuations. With cruise, you drive all day right at the limit. More miles per day means more dollars per day. We'd been told not to expect a jake brake or cruise control to be on our first truck; it was a perk on newer trucks for drivers with more longevity than C-teams.

The most important feature of a jake is its dependability down a mountain compared with brake shoes. If a driver starts down a mountain in too high a gear and rides the brake shoes all the way down, the brake pads get so hot they get slippery. After that, it's off to the races because there is no way to slow down enough to downshift. That's what those "runaway truck" exits are for in the western mountains. A jake doesn't get hot and slippery, but even with the jake, you have to slow down and start down hill in a low, slow gear.

Cruise control and jake brakes weren't part of my experience with Justin. Justin wouldn't let me turn on cruise control, and he believed students should practice how to slow down and downshift instead of relying on jake brakes. But that wasn't the only difference between the two instructors. They totally differed in their approach to meals, rules, and time behind the wheel. Ed did most of the driving in his truck while Justin did none in his. Justin always had me checking things in Schneider's reference manual, and Ed never referred to it once. As a matter of fact, just for fun, David kept track of some of Ed's advice which differed from the manual's.

Manual: Drain the fuel/water separator every time you fuel.

Ed: Don't ever drain the fuel/water separator because it has a heater in it to keep accumulated water from freezing.

Manual: Submit the signed bill of lading immediately after delivery for each load.

Ed: If you go on vacation, save a few bills of lading to submit during your vacation week so you will get a paycheck at the end of vacation. Smoothes out the cash flow.

Manual: Use the bump and run technique to select the proper gear prior to entering a turn.

Ed: If you are having trouble with downshifting, forget about the bump and run. Just leave it in the same gear, slip the clutch, or stop and start out in low.

Manual: Fill out your daily logs according to federal regulations.

Ed: There is no way you can drive to satisfy Schneider, the customer, and yourself and keep an accurate log book that satisfies federal regulations. You have to keep a logbook that shows legal hours, but you have to drive hours that get the job done.

Manual: Expect the engine rpm to drop approximately 300 rpm for each gear position.

Ed: The 10-speed transmission gears are so close together, there is almost no change in engine rpm from one gear to another. To prove this last point, he made David start out from a stoplight in tenth gear, pulling an empty 53 foot trailer, slipping the clutch like mad.

When they reached Ohio, David had a turn driving on US 30 all the way to Indiana. The first section in Ohio is two-lane and curvy. During the last ten miles before it widens to a freeway, a livestock truck, or "bull hauler" in truck lingo, appeared on David's tailgate. The posted limit was 55 mph. David was going 56 mph and couldn't go faster if he'd wanted to because Schneider at that time had a governor on the engine to make speeding impossible. The bull hauler, four feet behind David and getting closer, was going crazy because he couldn't pass. He was probably screaming something on his CB but David and Ed had theirs turned off. Finally, at the on-ramp to the freeway section he gunned it and got almost past before veering right and forcing David to take the shoulder. That shoulder was good hard blacktop so no harm was done. And David handled his first emergency. Glad it was him, not me. Score: Shelley one accident; David one road rage.

By the time I graduated from two weeks of road training, David had just finished his first. We were out of synch. It would be a welcome week at home to finish taxes, find someone to water the African violets, choose the right wardrobe for the winter/spring transition in the truck, write a will, etc. That fervor to have things in order just in case gripped me. I started a search for the safe deposit key, something I'd seen once in twelve years.

It was not to be. David had conned his way out of a second week with Ed. In some respects, I was relieved because this meant David knew how to do everything. I figured he was a quick study learning in one week what took others two. He could probably back up anywhere, anytime. I still couldn't back into anything without constant coaching. We'd be a great team, trained by professionals, ready to ride. He'd back up; I'd go forward. Move over, America.

Ready or not, here we come!

9

After road training, twelve of our original Green Bay classmates reunited at Schneider's Milwaukee operating center (OC) for one last two-day training period. We delighted one another with war stories about the instructors we'd just been on the road with for two weeks. It was no surprise to me that Justin was the best, if honesty is the measure. Everyone else learned tips on how to be clever with their log books, tips which weren't entirely on the up-and-up. These tricks weren't Schneider sanctioned, by any means. They were, instead, life-style choices made by these particular drivers, and in a free-wheeling way, passed on to the student in the passenger seat. What's more, David, to my horror, had done very little driving. His instructor was trying to pile on paid miles for his next paycheck so drove long and hard through the night while David dozed in the sleeper berth.

For two days, we learned new details about filling out paperwork and map-reading. But our final surprise came the last afternoon when they told us we were going to learn how to drive double-bottoms, known to drivers as "wiggle wagons." Now, this concept of double or even triple trailers always struck me as a stupid, dangerous idea. But

Schneider needed drivers to pull Kohl's department stores' doubles, and we were among the lucky few to try for this endorsement.

Wiggle wagons? Surely they were kidding. Nonetheless, we sat down to watch a video of wiggle wagons at work. I thought they'd be showing us how to hook up the extra set of wheels and how to turn corners with this super-long rig. But instead we saw wiggle wagons on a test track, out of control from turning too sharply or exiting a ramp too quickly, plus all the excitement of a fish-tailing wiggle wagon in high winds. Our teacher gave us his first-hand account of how it was impossible to feel the second trailer start to fish-tail (the only way to know it was to see it in the mirrors) and how once fish-tailing started, there was a right way and wrong way to correct it. At that point, my gums were starting to bleed and whatever he may have said was lost in the mire of anxiety.

Right after the video, we put on our winter coats and walked outside to the teacher's rig where he showed us how to couple and uncouple all this equipment. They weren't wasting any time explaining things about this unique set-up. First of all, it's obvious right away that you cannot back up a double-bottom rig because it would jackknife. Instead, you deliver it to a pull-through parking spot all hitched together. After the extra trailer is uncoupled, it can be hitched directly to a tractor and backed separately to a loading dock.

We stood around shivering, watching our instructor hitch together two trailers, called pups, using a special set of extra wheels on a dolly. The dolly is manhandled into alignment with the second pup and then the tractor with the first pup is backed up to the dolly. Again, the dolly is manhandled forward enough to hook its hitch on the back of the first pup. The dolly's landing gear is cranked up. Now the driver can back the tractor plus first pup with dolly assembly just enough to shove the dolly under the second pup to engage its king-pin. The equipment is massive, heavy and labor intensive. And you need to see it to understand it.

David was the first to drive the whole assembly around the block, and I was second. The tight spot on the training trip was a sharp right turn onto a frontage road where a penguin, one of those black and white posts, guarded a deep ditch at the edge of the shoulder. My turn came, and I screwed up enough courage to get through the moment and surprised myself. It was so easy. The second trailer followed the first one around the penguin just like a kid's toy train on the living room floor. Actually two short pup tandems handle a sharp corner better than a single 53' trailer.

After wiggle wagons, the class piled into two cars and drove to the nearby DOT office to pass the written test and add a "Tandem" endorsement to our CDL's. Best of all, we'd finished Schneider's final requirements that would allow us get a truck of our own.

All along, we'd considered accepting an offer to be dedicated drivers for one of Schneider's premium accounts, Kimberly-Clark. There were advantages to this plan including more miles per week, predictable routes and routine. But after a short sample during our two weeks of road training, we'd seen the Kimberly Highway as well as Baxter's dedicated run, and we were sure we'd rather see the world. We asked Schneider about letting us run the system instead.

Teams like us generally get assigned to loads with more distant destinations. There are constraints due to regularly scheduled time-at-home, but other than that there is no telling where you might be sent. Even exotic foreign countries, like Canada. We were itching to see everything, and Schneider made the change without hesitating. So we were licensed, endorsed, tested, measured, and weighed. We'd been given fuel credit cards and fuel stop books and atlases and reference guides. We'd been given everything but the key to the pumpkin truck. And within three days, that happened, too.

Our pumpkin was parked at the Schneider OC in West Memphis, Arkansas, and we were supposed to get there by bus. The good news was that the bus was a Schneider company bus, and the better news was that we were the only two passengers aboard -- all thirty-eight seats were ours.

Our personal driver for this trip was a veteran Greyhound driver named "J.B." Into his empty bus we piled our sleeping bags, duffel bags, food, computer, cameras, bird books, binoculars, cell phone, phone book, pillows, sheets, boots, jackets, briefcase, books-on-tape, water jugs, new toolbox, a crowbar that wouldn't fit in the new toolbox, empty laundry bag. J.B. smiled benevolently. He'd seen folks like us come and go, but probably with less stuff.

J.B. was seventy-three years old. A native Texan, he had claiming rights to an American Indian grandmother, a living mother in her nineties, long friendships with Mickey Mantle and Milton Berle, and trophies for winning two Professional Bowling Association tournaments in 1962. He pulled a yellowed newspaper from the glove compartment with an article that summed up his glory years and described a great old timer still respected in the bowling scene. In 1962 with $14,000 in the bank, he was happily supporting himself by hustling and tournaments.

After his bowling arm gave out, he operated a couple of successful businesses before retiring to a part-time job with Greyhound as a substitute bus driver. Then he saw the ad for this job, running the company bus back and forth between Dallas and Green Bay with occasional side trips to Memphis. He was known by name at every toll booth, convenience store, and the Charleston Inn in Charleston, Missouri where he stayed twice a week. That was his regular stop, and they saved him the same room and the same table on Fridays when they served their famous local catfish.

David spent hours in the front seat sharing the wisdom of J.B.'s fifty accident-free driving years. The secret, he said, was to leave your testosterone at home and forget about proving your manhood on the road. If someone cuts you off, back off and let him collide with someone else. Driving, he said, is just a way to get from here to there, not a defining moment in your life. He scoffed at speeders. And he certainly never warned drivers about speed traps. "Damn fools, they should all get tickets."

David knew he was the right person to be hearing this. He was susceptible to minor cases of road rage. In the car, he often showed an intolerance for drivers who barged in front of him at a stoplight or exit ramp. He'd race to head them off while I buried my head in my hands. Maybe J.B.'s wisdom would rub off.

It was a two-day trip to West Memphis, out of snow one day and into spring the next. By the time we reached the OC, we were in shirt sleeves and loving it. It was about fifty-five, twenty-five degrees warmer than Wisconsin, and it sure felt like spring. This truck driving life was looking up.

The fuel desk clerk directed us to maintenance where we each got a new set of truck keys. We found our cab-over tractor sitting in the long row of bobtails, a clone like all the others. J.B. pulled the bus alongside our new pumpkin coach, and we unloaded. Everything got spread out on the pavement while we emptied the previous driver's dregs from the two sideboxes (little compartments under the bunk, accessible from outside doors). We filled a carton with half-used isopropyl alcohol bottles, broken lights, water-logged log books, broken reflector triangles. While I fussed over house-cleaning, David fussed over the mechanical integrity of "Unit #19396." With a half million miles on the engine and another half-million to go before Schneider would trade her in, he was doing a pre-trip inspection right out of the Schneider guide. Brake linings, air lines, brake cylinders, belts, compressor, spring hangers -- that list again. It was clear that our new tractor needed a few critical items, but the most important breakdown to me was the non-functioning tachometer, a vital part of my shifting tool kit. Veteran drivers could shift by ear and instinct, but not me.

The only way I could shift was to watch the tach and shift either up or down at the appropriate rpm's. Far from foolproof even with the tach, without it, it was hopeless.

The clerk at the maintenance desk explained that tachs weren't on the list of priority items to be fixed for walk-in's like us, and that an item like that would have to wait another month for regular preventative maintenance there at the Memphis OC. I explained that unless the tach was fixed right then, the entire gear box would have to be replaced there at the Memphis OC. The clerk wasn't amused. Neither was I.

They fixed the tach. But they wouldn't fix the city horn, ever. It's one of two truck horns, the other being the air horn. Only brand new trucks had working city horns. This meant that a friendly tap of the horn to an absent-minded little old lady would be an air blast from hell instead of a sweet toot on a city horn.

Everything David could fix or oil himself, he fixed or oiled. We used the industrial-strength vacuum to suck out every trace of sand and dirt, every trace of the previous driver except the strong aroma of Marlboros. By now, stale cigarette smoke was molecularly bonded to the upholstery. Never in a million years could it be totally sucked out.

We washed the mirrors, the outside of the windows, the inside of the windows. They're so big, it's like washing the windows of a house. We stretched the fitted sheet over the mattress and found our regular-size fitted sheet was too short. Big trucks are over eight feet wide on the outside and the bunk fills the entire inside width. We nudged our belongings into every nook and cranny, defying laws of space and matter.

We turned on the truck computer and learned what had happened to the previous driver. A list of messages to and from his Service Team Leader (STL), or boss, moved across the screen:

"YOUR WIFE IN CAR ACCIDENT. SHE'S OK BUT WANTS YOU TO CALL IMMEDIATELY."

His message back:

"VERY SORRY MUST FIND WAY TO ST LOUIS IMMEDIATELY AND LEAVE TRUCK HERE IN W. MEMPHIS."

He didn't have time to delete the messages or leave his keys at the desk. So, there was a bit of reality.

That night, borrowing a company car (two were available free of charge for drivers' errands) we drove to Wal-Mart to buy some missing items. What possibly were we missing? David wanted to replace the truck's lousy radio with a removable car stereo. He wanted a model with a scanning button and clock, one that permanently told time instead of reverting back to the station call-sign. We still needed a cooler that plugged into the cigarette lighter, and Justin recommended a plug-in fan to circulate air in the sleeping area of the cab in hot weather. And David cannot be without a compass on the dash. Plus we were out of WD-40 and could use a mattress cover and sheets that fit.

Wal-Mart had everything but the right radio. In the cooler aisle, we bought a large-size Igloo that operated in either a conventional chest-type posture, or upright. All the king's men couldn't fit the amount of food we'd brought with us into this large-size Igloo. So we bought a couple of hanging nets that parents string over their kids' beds for stuffed toys and vowed to eat for dinner all the surplus food we couldn't refrigerate. Eventually, we bought a second smaller cooler for the excess.

We installed the balance of our belongings and new purchases around the bunk of a steadily shrinking truck. We would be developing an intimate acquaintance with the Igloo since the only place it fit was on the bed, David's side. Across the foot-end of the bed one net was strung diagonally and held important food like Rice Krispie Treats, cereals, crackers, Granola bars, peanut M&M's (later moved closer to the dashboard), popcorn, potato chips, etc. The other net, a heavier version made to keep things from blowing out the back end of a pick-up, held canned goods like tuna fish, Vienna sausages, corned beef hash, baked beans, lasagna, beef stew and replacement cans of potato chips. We stowed the gallon of cranberry juice in the sidebox, the large flashlight in the vinyl pocket on the door, the mini-flashlight in the visor, the compass on the dash, the paper towels on a bungee cord under the center visor, the fan in the sidebox until the weather changed.

In the visor pocket, we clipped the single-channel walkie-talkie (channel 14) David bought at Radio Shack. This item, he felt, would make backing up safer, and it really did. Into the drink holder molded in the dashboard panel, we placed the new water bottle with plastic straw. This purchase was designed to keep us from breaking a tooth as we bounced over the highway trying to drink. "Rides like a truck" makes it nearly impossible to drink straight from a juice bottle, especially on rough pavement.

Everything else from telephone books to computers fit around the three walls of the bed. Extra coats hung on two hooks David installed at the back behind the food nets. There was room for a person in a seat or in the middle of the bed, but no place else. Instantly, David wanted a conventional tractor with the engine in front, more room in the back, and began complaining about life as a spider, crawling over the dog house in the cab-over. It was too late because on Saturday we received our first assignment:

Take an empty trailer from the West Memphis OC to Procter and Gamble in Jackson, Tennessee. Pick up a loaded trailer (Pringle potato chips) by 10:00 Monday and deliver to Wal-Mart in Menomonie, WI by 22:00 Tuesday.

With an early start, David figured the route would take us right past Madison in time to drop in on the annual Academy Awards party our friends would be enjoying without us for the first time in fifteen years. Our maiden voyage and David, as he did throughout our driving life, jumped at the chance to turn routine into adventure. We didn't call our friends in Madison. David wanted to surprise them. Our car was parked at an official Schneider fuel stop just south of the city, a simple matter of parking the truck there, hopping in our car, and driving to the party for a few hours. Then we'd have a long nap, maybe in our own house, and all day Tuesday to drive to Menomonie.

We couldn't believe our good fortune.

We puttered around Saturday evening and looked for an empty trailer in the yard Sunday. We didn't need this empty trailer for our Pringles load (that was already loaded and waiting for us), so this was just Schneider's way of shuttling empty trailers, and Pringles needed a steady supply. Turned out, empty trailers were a rare commodity in the West Memphis OC that week. Four other drivers beside us waited twenty-four hours in vain. We parked right in the special empty trailer drop lot Sunday night in order to pounce on the first empty to come in. David sat up every time he heard a truck rumble by, but no empties arrived. By 07:00 Monday and time running out for our 10:00 deadline in Jackson, Green Bay let us get under way and pick up an empty across the muddy Mississippi at a logistics warehouse ten miles east of Memphis, Tennessee.

But the window of opportunity for a surprise appearance at the Academy Award party in Madison had closed. We'd just experienced our first frustration with scheduling, our first professional driver reality check. Now, instead of twenty-four extra hours for the trip and some time at home, we would barely meet our deadline – not because of weather, not because of traffic, not because of a union walk-out somewhere, but because Schneider couldn't fix us up with an empty trailer.

Finally, it was time to start earning a living. It was time to leave the sheltered world of Schneider parking lots and enter the American interstate highway system on our own. We nosed up to the exit gate, driver window cranked down, secret driver number memorized. A voice from the bull horn asked, "Driver number?"

"51379."

It took just a moment for that to find its way through the massive computer system.

"Have a safe trip, David." They knew who we were.

The barrier swung up and out of the way; we moved through it and into a new world. No office, ever again. The transformation from heavily supervised student to King of the Road happened in that instant. Schneider had tossed us the keys to their expensive truck and said, in effect, go on out there, do your best, and we'll expect your call in a couple of days in Wisconsin. The rest was up to us. We were on our own with a job to do anyway we thought best. If anybody was looking over our shoulder, it was our STL far away in Milwaukee watching our truck by satellite and waiting for our daily phone call. It's not exactly like a sea bird stepping off the cliff to take wing for the first time, but close.

David drove first. Sometimes he has a problem with getting his compass upside down. He pulled out of the OC about 07:30, went 1/4 mile north to pick-up I-40 and, anticipating a left turn instead of a right turn, missed the on-ramp. Since we were bobtailing, it was no big deal to get turned around and go back to the on-ramp, but this would have been a huge deal if we'd had a trailer.

To keep these screw-ups to a minimum, during the next few days one of us sat in the passenger seat calling out intersections, exit ramps, left or right turn, speed change, construction zone, you name it. The thought of calling a cop to direct traffic while we backed out of a dead end was horrifying.

But then, as we approached Procter and Gamble in Jackson, Tennessee, the compass reversed again, this time with an empty trailer in tow. Our instructions were to go through three stoplights and turn left. While I was reading a map, David turned at the third light instead of going through it, and we found ourselves heading down a narrow city street into a subdivision. Panicked, David veered into a convenience store with a large gravel parking lot that happened to be just big enough to turn around. We dodged another bullet and got back on track.

At Procter and Gamble, the guard took one look inside our empty trailer and declared it wasn't clean enough for Pringles. We had to pull over, sweep it out, slide the trailer tandems back to the 11th hole, then drop it in a numbered parking slot and pick-up our loaded trailer from another slot in the drop lot.

Now, sliding trailer tandems was something we'd read about, but only practiced once. Depending on the age and amount of rust under the trailer, the job is hard or even harder. Basically, you pull a lever under the trailer which frees the wheels to slide on a track either forward or backward and that allows you to balance the load front to back. (Think of a teeter-totter and how it's balanced.) A balanced load prevents wear and tear on state highways and is one of the things the DOT measures when trucks pull off the highway onto the scales. There's more about this later.

Cleaning the truck is where our purchases started paying off. The brand new Wal-Mart broom kept us in the guard's good graces. He frowned on drivers borrowing his personal broom. The hand-held single-channel CB radio let me stand near the empty slot on David's blind side and help talk him into it. His maiden solo backing assignment went smoothly, and we were out the gate with 23,000 pounds of Pringles, evenly balanced.

Even though we couldn't make it to the party in Madison that night, David was still determined to watch the Academy Awards on television somewhere. We consulted our brand new Interstate Exit Guide, an indispensable two-volume travel guide designed mainly for truck drivers. It tells what facilities, including truck parking, are available at every interstate highway exit in the United States. As we moved into central Illinois, temperatures had fallen to 10 above zero, so it was a pleasant surprise to find that the only motel with truck parking also had plug-ins to keep the engine from freezing. We parked in gear with the air brakes off so they wouldn't freeze up, plugged in the engine heater, checked in and went to the Oscars.

Next morning at 05:00, David went out to warm up the truck, but it wouldn't start. It wasn't completely dead, just too stiff to turn over fast enough to fire. This was going to be grim. The desk clerk suggested a place to call for a jump start, and they agreed to come after they caught up on all the other emergency calls for cold weather starts. The cost would be $50 to $100 and possibly our responsibility for not letting the engine idle all night.

There are many reasons why a truck won't start in cold weather. The oil gets stiff, maybe too stiff to allow the starter to crank it over. The batteries lose most of their cranking power. The fuel doesn't get hot enough to explode in the compression cycle. Half-frozen diesel fuel gets thick and it gels making it impossible to flow through the fuel pump. Water in the fuel freezes and blocks the flow of fuel somewhere between tank and combustion cylinder.

To fight this, we add alcohol to the fuel, remove water with the fuel/water separator, spray ether into the air intake during start, or plug in the engine heater. If the wrecker couldn't start the engine with jumper cables, then the whole truck would have to be towed to a warm garage for an hour to thaw the frozen water in the fuel lines.

David went back to try one last time, but this time he thought to hit the starter with his foot on the clutch. The engine started right up. It was another rookie mistake. No one ever mentioned the reason why you should start with a foot on the clutch except that it was safer than accidentally starting in gear. Now here was a second reason. The front half of the ice cold transmission puts too much drag on the engine for cold weather starting. He rushed to cancel the service call.

By afternoon we were pondering the twists and turns of fickle weather. Our route to Menomonie was on I-94. Littering the I-94 shoulder the last fifty miles before touchdown at Wal-Mart, we counted forty-eight cars and trucks that had spun off the road during a monumental blizzard the night before while we were sleeping safely in our motel room. Had our schedule been a little tighter with our delivery scheduled for early Tuesday morning instead of Tuesday afternoon, we'd have been in the middle of that mess on our very first delivery.

Instead the interstate was salted and safe, and we arrived at Wal-Mart's warehouse, a fenced fortress with guardhouses and uniformed guards who inspected tamper-proof metal seals locked on our trailer doors back in Jackson. They directed us to a numbered slot in a yard as big as an airport where we dropped the trailer. Our next assignment was already beeping on the computer before we finished cranking down the landing gear on this first load of Pringles.

It took us to Eau Claire, Wisconsin, to a Nestle factory, where we hooked up to a 53' trailer loaded with 43,000 pounds of infant formula. Inside, everything was swaddled in quilted blankets to keep the cans from freezing. Our first freezable load, the bill of lading warned, "Keep above 50 degrees Fahrenheit." The theory is that once the trailer is moving, jostling keeps the liquid from freezing. If we stopped for long, we'd have to find a trailer heater to put in with the formula. Trailer heater was never mentioned in school; we had no idea what it was.

Forty-seven-thousand pounds is about the maximum a trailer can carry before the whole truck exceeds the 80,000 pound maximum. So with 43,000 pounds of milk inside and a huge snow drift on top of the trailer from the blizzard the day before, we had to get the truck weighed to make sure the tandems were in the right holes, and the load was balanced. A truck scale two miles from Nestle gave us the bad news: 80,560 pounds gross weight and 36,400 on the trailer tandems. We weren't legal regardless of what hole the tandems were in.

All that snow and ice on the trailer had to weigh at least 560 pounds. If we found a truck wash to hose it off, we could probably weigh-in less than 80,000 pounds, but the trailer axles had to lose another 2,000 pounds! Was that possible? The nearest truck wash was back up I-94 at Menomonie, but there was a DOT scale between us and it. Did we really want to sneak by on county roads still slippery from the recent blizzard?

We called Schneider for advice. The night shift advised us to head south fifty miles to a truck wash at Black River Falls. No DOT scale in that direction, and Schneider would pick up the $50 wash ticket. On the way to Black River Falls most of the two foot snow drift blew off the top, but the ice remained. We pulled into the automatic wash stall, and the attendant warned as he pointed above to a row of nozzles, "Is everything rolled up tight? There's 350 gallons per minute shooting out of this thing."

We checked the windows and vents, crawled in the back to take a catnap, not expecting what the machine-gun drumming of high pressure water jets on the hollow cab would sound like. Too late, we were trapped inside. It took half an hour of sweeping back and forth over the trailer top with a phalanx of high volume, high pressure nozzles to melt and knock off the thick layer of ice. In addition, other nozzles attacked the sides and undercarriage. When it was all over we weighed 74,900 pounds. Was it possible to wash off three tons of ice or were the truck stop scales wrong?

We'd also washed off the work light on the cab and burned out a side light on the tractor. With a coupon from the truck wash for a free steak dinner we took time to eat, time to think up lots of things to worry about. We worried about the infant formula and brakes freezing in the near zero temperatures. We debated whether to take the time to get the lights fixed and whether to get re-weighed. Still wondering whether we actually melted three tons of ice off the truck, David questioned if somehow he had been parked wrong on the scale, another rookie mistake?

He talked to the manager, and they examined the scale to make sure it was still "zeroed." Nothing was wrong with the scale, but we decided to get back in the truck and have it re-weighed anyway, but by then, the wash water in the tractor's door locks had frozen hard as a rock. The maintenance garage loaned us their propane torch.

David got a door key as hot as he could and pushed it into the keyhole to thaw the lock. After a few tries, we were back in the truck again and out of the frigid weather.

The brake shoes were not yet frozen to the drums, but it would have served us right if they had been. We should never have parked with the parking brake on. We stuck another $10 bill in the scale, and out came another ticket showing 74,900 pounds. We were legal and on our way to Baxter Health Care in Waukegan.

Our learning curve was underway; our first delivery was over. Our second delivery and our careers had just begun. David called his kids from the next truck stop. I overheard him say, "It's not exactly like being on vacation, but it sure isn't exactly like work either."

10

As it happened, life in the truck got off to a shaky start. Strike that: make it a volcanic start. David and I thought we knew what it was like to work joined at the hip. After all, we'd been in close quarters on the boat for eight months and lived to tell about it. Except for anchoring, life was bliss. And we'd been in business together. Except for almost going bankrupt, we lived to tell about it. So I expected in this dream job there would be rough times, disagreements, friction just as in any happy marriage. You cope.

But in the truck, we broke new ground. David put it this way: "We're peeling back the foreskin of domestic bliss."

My husband, not a patient man, had nowhere to go with his impatience other than the sleeper berth, two feet behind my head. That wasn't far enough. He'd yell at my crappy shifting. And over the roaring diesel, he could hear me screaming back like a banshee. Whatever reconciliation tools we'd forged in twenty years of marriage turned into clubs. Every little resentment, and some weren't so little, was made worse by being tired, hungry, lost, frightened, insecure, or having to pee.

Whatever David's faults, incompetence was never one of them. He could do anything — at least I used to think so. So as he became infuriated with my incompetence, I began to pick on his. The goddamn guy continued to get right and left so mixed up that he'd get us hopelessly lost, not once, but dozens of times. Typically, it happened at interstate truck stops where he'd negotiate a set of turns to get in somewhere and then forget how to get back out. Instead of getting back on the interstate, we'd be chugging down some road looking for a place to turn around. I'd be stuck in the bunk trying to fall back to sleep and would feel the truck turn the wrong way — too late to say anything. If it wasn't such a disaster getting lost, it would have been funny. But funny it wasn't.

So I was determined that the next time we were at home, I'd stay there. It was an idle threat, but David eventually got a chance to leave me behind. His journal, a bunch of letters he emailed to his kids, began with this one:

Subject: First solo

Spent a busy weekend at home May 24 - 26. Then Shelley flew to Princeton for son's graduation, and I began my solo stint. Set the alarm for 04:00 so I could drive a car to Stoughton where we'd parked the loaded truck, refuel it, and drive it to Mazomanie, Wisconsin, for a 07:00 appointment.

Arrived only fifteen minutes late. Was assigned a receiving dock and a pallet jack to use to unload the truck. I set to work, and the first third of the load went quickly because the cartons were all on pallets. That's because I had requested pallets during the loading process a few days earlier in Holyoke, Massachusetts.

But the two-thirds of the trailer containing five hundred cartons of Tampax and Jergens lotion samples had to be re-stacked by hand, by me, onto pallets for handling in the Roundy's warehouse. That exercise kept me sweating until 12:30. Sure would have been nicer with Shelley there.

My next assignment took me to Prairie du Chien at the confluence of the Mississippi and Wisconsin rivers. I chose a route along the Wisconsin River through small towns, hilly farm and woodland country. Took two wrong turns that required some creative and risky maneuvers in order to recover. Crossed a surprise fifteen-ton bridge. Had no one to say, "Gee, look at the sandstone cliff over there." Sure would have been nicer with Shelley there.

At 3M in Prairie du Chien the paperwork for my shipment of flammable cleaning supplies to Philadelphia was lost. A few phone calls to Schneider cleared that up. My load was still there. The previous driver had just taken the paperwork.

Sure enough, a search of the yard was fruitful and I finally got out of there about 18:00 with my first load of hazardous materials. But now time was short. Schneider hadn't planned on the Roundy's unload taking so much time, or the snafu at 3M either. So the Philadelphia load with a firm deadline of 06:00 next day would require all night driving. Special notes for this consignee included, "No late deliveries. Many service failures on this account. No late deliveries!" Sure would have been nicer with Shelley there.

I looked in the Schneider trip planning guide for the recommended route from Wisconsin to Philadelphia and followed that route. It took me the length of Pennsylvania on I-80, then southeast on an extension of the Pennsylvania Turnpike to Philly. In central Pennsylvania about midnight I took a two-hour nap and pressed on. After an hour I needed another hour nap. At that point I figured I had four hours left to drive four hours. Somehow my trip plan had been off by two and a half hours. I should have been much closer by then. Sure would have been nice to have Shelley there.

Then a dangerous situation developed. On the CB I heard someone say, "Four-wheeler on the shoulder." Didn't pay much attention, but topping a hill there was the 4-wheeler backing down the shoulder to get back to an exit he missed with half the car-width in my eastbound lane. As luck would have it, a semi was passing me at that moment so I couldn't swerve into the left lane, and it was too late to stop. I squeezed as far left as I dared in the split seconds available, balancing the risk of scraping the passing semi against the risk of wiping out the family in the small car. Was that a "thump" I heard back around the trailer wheels or just my imagination? Next thing I heard on the CB was a trucker reporting the same 4-wheeler still on the shoulder. I kept going. If I'd touched him it was only to rip off a mirror, and it served him right. I wasn't going to risk my life stopping on the freeway after midnight to walk around comforting that fool. It's illegal to stop and back up on the freeway. It's stupid to do so in the lane of traffic. I kept telling myself it's not my fault.

At 05:00 charging down the turnpike extension in the mountains near Allentown, the following sign appeared: "Tunnel 5 miles, poisonous or flammable liquid prohibited." On all four sides of my trailer there were twelve-inch square, bright red placards with the word "FLAMMABLE" which were sure to attract the attention of the tunnel attendants and State Patrol cars that hang around tunnels. Arrest, fines, inquiries, humiliation. Now what?

I tend not to worry about special risks like a hazardous material load. I hadn't called anyone at Schneider to ask for help in trip planning. I hadn't read the Pennsylvania trucking guide that explains the ban on flammable liquids on turnpikes and in tunnels. That's Shelley's specialty. She would have been very worried about the flammable stuff and would have made plenty of inquiries and would have figured out a legal route. She also would have been suspicious that the Schneider route was one hundred twenty-five miles longer than the paid mileage figure I had been using. Sure would have been nice to have had that help twelve hours earlier.

There was no time to jump off at the next exit, get out the maps and plan a new route through the mountains near Allentown. I'd be hours late. It's okay to refuse or re-negotiate a delivery time at the beginning of a trip. To call three hours before deadline and say it's unsafe and impossible would have cost me my month's bonus and Schneider's relationship with the customer. Only five minutes left to come up with a plan.

Two miles before the tunnel, on a wide section of shoulder with no flood lights, I parked the truck and ran around ripping off the "FLAMMABLE" placards. Quick, before anyone came along, I jumped back on the turnpike, knees shaking, and zipped through that tunnel and the next one with an illegally marked trailer, but one that attracted no attention whatsoever. I'd chosen a double violation instead of the single tunnel violation, but one where I was less likely to be caught. Sure glad Shelley wasn't there.

The delivery in Philly was one of those difficult parking situations where I had to sneak through a parking lot full of cars, turn back onto the street, then back down into a dark garage off the narrow residential street. When Shelley is there, she keeps me on track with encouragement and instructions on the portable CB radio. Sure would have been nicer with Shelley there.

Next stop was a drop lot in a Philadelphia suburb to pick up a shorter 48' trailer. There were two, both with flat tires. I bobtailed to a nice diner, treated myself to a hot meal, returned to the drop lot to hook up one of the bad trailers. Another driver filled my ear with his tale of woe. His assignment was to pick up a certain trailer in the lot, but it was buried behind four others that would have to be moved first. I wished I could have helped him move trailers around that congested lot, but with three hours sleep in the last thirty and only three hours to fix the flat and get to the next pick up, I was in no mood to add to my work load. Next stop was a Goodyear shop not far away to get a tire changed. Next stop was a plastics factory near Camden, New Jersey, to pick-up a load of raw plastic pellets for the Bemis toilet seat factory in Sheboygan Falls, Wisconsin. And then it was close to rush hour in Philadelphia. No time to nap, time to rush through the middle of Philly at the beginning of rush hour to try to beat the big rush. Wondered if Shelley was having a swell time in Princeton. Bill Clinton was the graduation speaker.

To keep my logbook legal, I hadn't been filling it out until enough delays at delivery docks and drop lots were accumulated so I could show the required eight-hour rest period between ten-hour driving periods. I logged the trip to Prairie du Chien, for instance, as happening immediately after arrival at Roundy's so the unloading hours could be used to log a rest period that afternoon after all the Wisconsin driving hours. The time spent driving all over Philadelphia I just logged as a rest period in Philadelphia. So as I started west on the Pennsylvania Turnpike, my log showed I was well-rested when, in reality, I was pretty tired from almost constant work for thirty-six hours. It's called cheating and even though Shelley would have given me shit, it would have been nicer with her there.

Safely out of Philadelphia rush hour traffic, I pulled over and took a long nap. Then pressed on to the Schneider truck stop at Akron, Ohio, where I got my first night of real sleep in two days. Next day, cruising down I-71, gabbing with other drivers on the CB about the woman driver in the station wagon and the 4-wheeler that made a U-turn across the median and got caught by a Smoky Bear, I blew past my exit by about twenty miles. Had to cut across Ohio on some state roads to get back on track. At one point I had to do some map reading. As a team member I was used to asking my partner to study the map and call out the route, but now I had to park the truck in a small town and study the map before getting too far down the wrong road again. Hastily pulled into a small, vacant parking lot that turned into the customer parking for a small drive-through bank. It wasn't closed, just a slow day with no customers' cars in the lot just then. I read the map and quickly got out of there, but not before dragging my trailer wheels across some very green, very wet sod. Again, visions of damage complaints, inquiries, lost bonus. Sure would have been nicer with Shelley there.

Cut my next rest period short in order to beat the morning rush hour in Chicago, but mistimed it and got to Gary about 07:00. Had a shower and big breakfast and watched Forrest Gump in the Schneider OC, waiting long enough to let traffic die down until 10:00 before giving it a try. By then I only had four hours left to cover the final miles to the next delivery deadline, so needed some luck to avoid any big traffic jams. Made it with five minutes to spare.

From there, Schneider took me to Norway in Upper Michigan to get a load of paper pulp at Champion Paper. Something had happened to the pulp-making ability at their South Carolina paper mill, and they were shipping pulp to South Carolina by every means available including trains. I saw at least thirty Schneider truck loads on the schedule board. I headed back south again about sun set. Kept going until midnight when a local driver helped me find the entrance to a truck stop in the dark rainy night off the US-41 freeway. Grabbed four hours sleep there, then veered west a little bit to pick up Shelley at home. The rest of the trip to South Carolina sure was a lot nicer.

So much for following rules and weeks of book-learning. Getting lost was a huge hairball, but it was rookie me who nearly got someone killed with a bunch of shifting errors and misjudgments. Late one night on the Pennsylvania Turnpike, David had parked us for a few hours of sleep with the alarm set. When it went off, my turn to drive came, and I jumped up, half dead. I knew we were against a tight deadline, and I didn't take any time to fill in the logbook, wake up, or think straight. We were parked in a typical obsolete turnpike truck turn-off, nothing more than a black cinder clearing where trucks lined up parallel to one another. Having arrived late at night, the only place left for David to park was toward the far end of the clearing on an upgrade. So when I idled off in second gear, I was going uphill with almost no room in front of me to get up enough speed to pull out onto the highway. Even though I'd watched the oncoming traffic for several minutes waiting for a gap in which to merge, that gap was not infinite. I knew I was in trouble when the first shift went badly. By the time I was in the driving lane, I was totally intimidated, flustered and stalled to a stop. Even at that time of the early morning, the turnpike had plenty of traffic. So there I was dead stopped in a busy lane of traffic scrambling for second gear all over again. Trucks were roaring up behind me, swerving to get into the passing lane, air horns blasting. David woke up immediately, yelled at me to turn on the flashers, talked me through the whole starting and shifting procedure; there's no question whatsoever that we could have been rear-ended. He was furious and had every reason to be.

He got over it, and I got better because during the next three years we drove over half a million miles — enough to circle the globe twenty times — without killing anyone or getting killed ourselves. We had near misses, some serious enough to have killed us. But they didn't. Assignments took us to every state and Canada. Not only did the view out our office window change minute to minute, but the seasons began earlier and ended later as we'd travel south, then north and back south again. Sometimes we'd go from spring to winter in a day, or vice versa. However bad the weather, we knew we'd be out of it in a day or two. Weather was never routine.

Keeping the job user-friendly was the goal. Every team has its own requirements, and usually that's making money. Ours wasn't. We wanted adventure — legal and safe — and getting paid for it was a welcome bonus. We were willing to come within the acceptable but lower end of Schneider's expectations for team driver miles just to keep the adventure part alive.

Schneider assignments led us through hot California deserts in the dead of winter, cool Colorado alpine meadows in summer or, switching directions and seasons, through scorching Arizona deserts in summer and ice cold North Dakota in a blizzard. We were no strangers to headliner ice storms in Maine, hundreds of miles of treeless plains in Nebraska and bridges over most of the country's big rivers. Looking down at the Mississippi, Hudson, Columbia, Snake, Missouri, Arkansas, Ohio, Colorado, and Columbia from the panoramic window of a big truck was like having free season's tickets to an Imax theater. It made us appreciate the country's scenic river system in ways that would otherwise have taken years of expensive vacation road trips. The engineering miracle of colossal bridges over the Straits of Mackinaw, Chesapeake Bay, San Francisco Bay, Columbia River gorge, Boulder Dam, even the Golden Gate are much more interesting when you're sitting up high enough to see over the guard rail.

We traveled to off-beat places using Schneider as not only our employer, but as our travel agent. By managing our time and by doing our homework, we uncovered adventures, some big and some small, on almost every trip. We saw three films at the Sundance Film Festival in Park City, Utah; went to Sea World in San Diego where we parked the tractor next to RVs bigger than we were; toured the Hearst Castle (San Simeon) and both Getty Museums in California; spent a weekend on Tybee Island, Georgia, in a quaint oceanside guest house with a sandy parking spot just big enough for our bobtail; toured historic Old Albuquerque in New Mexico; camped overnight in California's Anza-Borrego desert park; ate great buffet meals at fantastic Las Vegas casinos at fantastically cheap prices; crossed the border at Nogales to shop for Mexican trinkets. And that's just the short part of a long list.

Our family, stretched out across the country coast to coast, never saw so much of us. We made regular stops to visit David's sister near Sacramento, just a short drive from our regular Schneider drop lot. We normally saw Molly once every other year, but now we'd visit six times a year. Other stops included a brother in Washington who found, two blocks from his house, a grocery store willing to let us park in their lot anytime; kids in Seattle who scouted out a side-street in an industrial area where we could safely leave a truck for a few hours; grandchildren in Massachusetts, where a small-town fire station let us park overnight; cousins in Los Angeles who picked us up at a Schneider drop lot and took us to a festive lunch; high-school friends living in Tucson; an elderly aunt in Ft. Lauderdale; parents in rural Pennsylvania; and close friends in Philadelphia, Boston, Montana and New Hampshire, many of whom we wouldn't have seen otherwise. Some of these visits were short – just a couple of hours – but plenty long enough to re-connect face-to-face and for free, and some were overnight.

This is what David wrote in an email.

Subject: Truckers at play

Here we are on a four-week trip. Normally we're gone two weeks then home one week. But in order to be home for the annual Academy awards party, we've arranged to stay away four weeks, then be home two weeks starting about March 18th.

Don't feel too sorry for us. After a quick trip from Wisconsin to Los Angeles via I-80 — which runs through Grand Island, Nebraska, and is the site at this time of year for the Sandhill crane/Canada goose/Snow goose mass (and we do mean *mass*) migration — we were picked up by my cousins at the Schneider drop lot and taken out to dinner. Only see them rarely and it's not often enough.

Next assignment took us from Los Angeles to Miami, an ideal winter trip with only 8,000 pounds of Easter baskets. Fuel economy soared to 8.3 miles per gallon -- 1,400 miles between fuel stops. The deserts are turning green after liberal El Nino rains. Local newspapers say it's the best blooming in twenty years. A thin blush of green fuzz covers desert gravels between ocotillo and cholla cactus all the way from Victorville, California, to west Texas. Flowers are just now starting to bloom.

In Florida we wanted to visit Shelley's ninety-one year old aunt in Deerfield Beach. Last visit was in 1979. Just by good luck, the deadline for delivering the Miami load had an extra day and a half of time available. By studying the motel coupon book and working the phones we lined up a West Palm Beach motel room for Tuesday and Wednesday night with big truck parking. Such facilities are rare in those parts as you can imagine. Got there late Tuesday night. Next morning took the motel shuttle to the airport, rented a car and drove the beach road from Palm Beach to Deerfield Beach.

Got another assignment. Took a skinny road up the east side of Lake Okeechobee through the sugar cane plantations which stretch forever like the wheat fields of Kansas. Lots of egrets and vultures. An occasional wood stork and white ibis — even a number of glossy ibis decorate the ditches. The load wasn't ready to pick up so we had time to finally see a movie, have a beer and a bite at Ruby Tuesdays in the fabulous "Florida's Mall."

In the early morning, picked up a load of pea-gravel for aquariums which was dyed pretty colors and packaged in a tiny backyard factory employing about six people. While they loaded the truck, we took a walk around the shabby, industrial/residential neighborhood. There was an Orange County sheriff's department Boot Camp with a forty-foot climbing tower for the Swat Team trainees to shinny up and down. They were busy marching in lock-step while an osprey worked in vain to build a sticky nest atop a single protruding 10" diameter round post.

Next we were on our way to Hattiesburg, Mississippi, through genuine bayou country with Cajun music on our FM radio. Had time in Hattiesburg for catfish, hushpuppies and collard greens. Even had time for cornbread and peach cobbler before catching a movie at a multiplex with good tractor parking.

Now we're visiting friends in Lafayette Hill, Pennsylvania, which we're passing on our way to drop our load of Kimberly-Clark paper napkins. Then we'll head west to Los Angeles where the green hills will be even greener and the beaches even warmer than our last visit two weeks ago.

Try this from your office!

11

Before you run right out and get your CDL, let me tell you about the times this easy job was hard work. First, try dealing with stuck landing gear in knee-deep mud in the middle of a rainy night with a dead flashlight. Imagine getting swept up in hours of Chicago freeway traffic with no place to stop and an overpowering urge to take a leak. Think about what it's like stopped halfway between the shoulder and driving lane, putting on tire chains in a mountain blizzard and hoping like hell you won't get rear-ended by another slip-sliding semi. Picture yourself getting up to drive after three hours of sleep at 03:00 am with the cab temperature below freezing, the sleeping bag warm, and the delivery deadline closing in.

Come along on this coast-to-coast trip:

Subject: Typical trip

Thursday, July 25, our truck needed its regular 20,000 mile physical so we scheduled it for 22:00 at the Schneider OC in Montebello, California, a suburb of Los Angeles. This was very convenient since we were dropping our load of transformers from Oshkosh, Wisconsin, there anyway. Truck maintenance takes about eight hours, and Schneider pays for our motel room if the work takes place overnight. Making sure to schedule maintenance overnight rather than during the day is part of the trip planning process because a free night in a motel is a nice prize after seventy-two hours in the truck. Especially this time because our air conditioner let us down again in the Mojave Desert where it's failed five out of seven times.

So, Friday morning we got a slow start. Called our scheduler about 09:30 from the motel to see if a new load had been assigned. Peggy reported that she had pushed us back to a 12:00 noon availability time because Shelley's name had popped up on the random drug-screening program, and Shelley had to report to a testing clinic ASAP to have her breath and urine analyzed.

We checked out, got delivered to the OC by the motel van, borrowed the company car, and drove a few miles to the walk-in clinic. The clinic was very industrial looking with an aluminum tread plate bolted to the front of the reception desk and nickel-plated wire-form chairs in the waiting room. It's big business handling referrals for employment physicals and substance abuse testing.

Shelley finished, and we returned to the OC where we learned the truck was ready except that it hadn't been washed. We were tempted to get underway in a dirty truck, but our last truck wash had been six weeks earlier, so we allowed the wash guy to take the keys while we bought authentic burritos from the roving lunch wagon making the industrial rounds.

A half hour later, it turned out the washing guy had gone to lunch also. Meanwhile, we were frustrated not to know our new assignment because the truck was waiting to be washed under a sheet metal roof and couldn't receive satellite signals. At 13:00 we found the wash guy installing a new wash chemical system but prevailed upon him to do that later and finish our truck first.

To save time, we went to the office computer and got a print-out of our new assignment. East eleven miles to the City of Industry to get a 53' empty trailer; west twenty-one miles to drop the empty and pick up a loaded one from the Sears facility in Vernon. Then 2,676 miles to a Sears distribution point in Wilkes Barre, PA, by

18:00 July 29th (three days drive). We average 850 miles per day, so there was barely enough time if we got an early start from Los Angeles. If we left by 15:00 we'd have exactly three days for the trip. If you do the math, at 850 miles per day we'd need three days plus 2.5 hours, so we were already late and would have to make up time on the trip.

Since it was a light load, we could zip through the short but mountainous Denver route. We'd go through Nevada just in time to gulp down $3.95 prime rib dinners at a casino. We'd hit the Rockies in daylight and take I-70 through Kansas, one of the six states we hadn't visited.

We filled the clean truck with diesel and left the OC ninety minutes later than the Schneider computer had predicted. And, as often happens, there was no empty trailer at the City of Industry drop lot. We'd driven forty-five minutes out the Pomona freeway for nothing. Phoned Schneider, waited another half hour, and got the message to drive twenty-five miles back in to central Los Angeles to get a specific trailer at the Southern Pacific truck/rail yard. Maybe this was a good sign. If Schneider has a specific trailer in mind, they must know it's there.

Back on the Pomona freeway with rush hour traffic crawling slowly in the opposite direction, we jumped onto I-5 downtown, jumped off and wove through narrow streets in bombed-out neighborhoods to the rail yard where there's a good view of the county jail. Waited in line to be checked through security into the yard. Carefully checked two hundred trailers for our specific trailer number. It wasn't there, no unlocked empties were there, and the regular drivers we spoke to didn't think there were ever empties there. It's a place for full trailers to hand off from rail to highway or highway to rail. Not a place to load and unload. What was Schneider thinking?

Now time was really getting short. Called Schneider again. Said the load was getting a late start and was beyond our usual 850 mile per day schedule. Any time spent chasing after phantom trailers would make it even later.

Scheduler said to wait thirty minutes to see if the computer assigned a new trailer. Got a ten minute nap with a hot breeze through open windows before the satellite beeped and advised us to forget the empty trailer search and bobtail directly to Sears.

The Sears warehouse is in Vernon, halfway toward Watts and a few minutes south of the Southern Pacific truck/rail yard. As long as they have security, California warehouses like Sears can get away with buildings that have no walls to keep out rain. The huge building stockpiled with supplies in the middle away from rain sat under a roof supported only by posts. A free-standing mobile home sitting in the center was the office. All around the property boundary was chain-link fence topped with tight loops of prison yard razor wire. Friday after 17:00 it was pretty empty there but we found someone in charge sleeping in the mobile home, found our trailer and discovered the landing gear was jammed and we could not couple to it.

Went back to the clerk in charge to ask if the yard hustler truck could help us out by lifting the nose of the trailer so we could get the landing gear crank un-jammed. He called around and learned the hustler was out getting fuel, would return in fifteen minutes, move a lot of important trailers first, then be available to help us. This was our only hope — other than to wait until Monday morning for the regular shift to return. The clerk in charge suddenly had a change of heart, jumped into a fork lift, drove out to our trailer and took enough weight off the landing gear for me to break it free.

By the time we connected, brought logbooks up to date and pointed east it was 18:30 California time, 21:30 in Wilkes Barre. We advised customer service we would be at least four hours late in Pennsylvania, they answered back to take fourteen hours and deliver by 08:00 July 30 instead. That was a cushion on the delivery end. It also meant we might get that prime rib dinner but not much before midnight with Los Angeles rush hour still in front of us. At least we'd have time to make some tourist stops along the way and use four or five hours each night to stop the truck and get real sleep. A tight schedule is exhausting — a loose schedule is a paid vacation.

Vernon, where Sears is, is a melting pot. As you drive along Atlantic Boulevard, the signs rotate through Spanish, Chinese, and Korean. I was starving. It was tempting to park and try a small diner, grocery or deli. Instead, Shelley fixed me a liver sausage sandwich with sweet pickle from our Coleman electric cooler while I drove and we got out of town.

I-15 to Las Vegas was packed with trucks and gamblers heading there for the weekend. It's a great sight to top a hill and see in the mirrors twenty miles of solid headlights all the way back to the sunset horizon. Climbing out between the San Gabriel and San Bernardino mountains went very quickly with our 14,574 pound load of "FAK" (freight of all kinds).

It had been a long day. I gave out and shut down about 22:00 at a rural exit called Zzyzx Road on I-15 near Baker, California. It was a stifling ninety degrees. Other trucking companies pay for fuel to keep the truck engine (and heater/air conditioner) idling all night if it's too hot or too cold. Not Schneider. Unless it's below +10 degrees F, our truck automatically shut down after five minutes of idling.

Shelley tried to keep sleeping, but as the air conditioning quickly wore off, she quickly got steamed, struggled to the driver's seat and got us rolling again.

Next I knew it was 05:30 Saturday morning. Before crawling back to bed, too tired to set the alarm clock, Shelley had driven only forty miles east but another 1,500 feet higher to a brake check area at the top of a pass. At that elevation the breezy nighttime temperature was a refreshing eighty degrees — world-class sleeping conditions. But now we were squandering time. We normally try to get four hours of motionless sleep but it had been over six. I struggled up and out of the truck in a cool drizzle, gave a cactus some extra moisture, and rolled toward the East.

Next time we stopped, I did my normal walk-around with the hammer checking tires and son-of-a-gun, found a flat one. It was one of the tractor tandems, so we stopped in Las Vegas where Schneider has an open account at a truck stop.

I parked right where the tire shop guy told me to, and it looked like he was available to start on a quick half-hour job. But an hour later I found myself complaining to the cashier about how much time the tire guy spent with his hands on his hips gossiping with Gary, and how little time he spent actually changing my tire.

Since Gary happened to be standing right beside me at the time, everyone apologized, and the tire job proceeded without interruption.

The flat had consumed another hour and a half of driving time which, added to the casino stop, the extra sleep last night, the running around Los Angeles on phantom trailer searches and the slow truck wash all added up to about seven hours behind schedule. Half our fourteen-hour cushion was gone already.

But what a trip lay ahead through Utah. Starts with the Virgin River Gorge just east of Mesquite, Nevada. Continues past Zion and Bryce Canyon National Parks. Like a symphony, it builds movement by movement to a climax as you drop down through several gold and bright red canyons to the San Rafael River valley. Not to be played after dark if you can help it.

We did end up in the Colorado Rockies after dark -- wonderful because a full moon backlit the canyon walls and mountain peaks. I was still going strong at 01:00 but parked and slept like a tourist just after the Eisenhower Tunnel at a cross road exit ramp. Cool temperatures, full moon, sound of water falling in the dark spruce woods.

Early Sunday I tried to get to the fuel stop in Denver without waking Shelley and missed the exit. Spent twenty minutes driving around a bad part of town looking for a way back across lots of railroad tracks to the fuel stop where we revived with the first shower in two days.

After Denver it's all down hill in more ways than one. Eastern Colorado, Kansas, Missouri, Illinois, Indiana, Indianapolis, Columbus, Akron, Youngstown. Pretty flat farm land. Slept in an Illinois rest area Sunday night and stopped in at the Indianapolis Schneider OC for food and fuel Monday morning. Good biscuits and gravy.

By 07:45 Monday we were on the home stretch out of Indianapolis. I-80 across Pennsylvania is a scenic, yet bad, road. Very busy with big trucks. Sixty-five mph is legal speed for trucks so naturally they go seventy or seventy-five. It's rough pavement, hilly, curvy. Four months ago the hills worried me a lot more than they do now after a half dozen trips west.

By the time we got to Wilkes Barre, we had our next assignment. From Wilkes Barre we would bobtail down to the edge of the Hackensack River in Jersey City to pick up a loaded trailer and take it 2,862 miles to French Camp near Sacramento. We like going west.

Meanwhile, we were learning more about the composition of Schneider's fleet. The company stayed out of the LTL (less than truckload), teamster-dominated business in which drivers travel between their sorting and distribution terminals, usually on the same route, with time at home after each round trip. Drivers "hot sheet" the cab, always keeping the truck moving just by switching drivers. Sometimes they drive day cabs, sometimes regular tractors, but it was never assigned to a single driver to keep clean, call his own, and move into.

The trailers we hauled were all vans. Those are the typical boxcars, totally enclosed to carry almost anything and keep it dry. Walls are aluminum and fiberglass which keeps the overall weight down. Floors are oak, laid up like a bowling alley's, so blocking can be nailed into it to prevent loads from shifting. It's the driver's cleanup job to pry all the bent, cement-coated nails out of the oak with a crowbar; often it's easier to break them off flush.

Vans are loaded and unloaded through rear double doors at a dock the same height as the trailer floor. Sometimes we unloaded the vans using hydraulic pallet jacks to move the pallets out onto the warehouse floor. It was good exercise, and we were paid extra for these driver-unloads. But usually we just dropped the trailer in the consignee's yard, or we opened the doors and backed it up to the dock and left it for warehouse personnel to unload. A rookie mistake is to back up to the dock without opening the doors first. That's a good way to park a trailer if you're worried about pilfering, but not a good way to park for unloading. If anyone's watching, it's good for a laugh.

If we needed the empty trailer because empties in the area were scarce, we'd wait while the receiver unloaded ours, meanwhile trying to catch a rollicking cat-nap in the cab while the fork-lift bounced in and out. We lived in a cab-over pumpkin truck for the first fourteen months, almost unheard of for team drivers today. It was like living in a pup tent, and David hated it.

But we needed seniority to get a better, bigger, newer truck, something we didn't have. Without seniority, there was only one other way. After David's persistent requests, Schneider finally called to offer us a conventional if we would just help them meet their commitment to have several new teams working exclusively (a "dedicated" account) for Toro Lawnmower until June. We got our conventional and for two months wore a groove between Toro factories in Tomah and Baraboo, Wisconsin, Minneapolis, and Memphis.

Subject: Dedicated to Toro

In early April our lives changed. In April we agreed to be scheduled 100% by Toro, the lawnmower company, for their busy season April and May. Schneider had contracted with Toro to supply a certain number of teams and was so eager for us to do this, they gave us one of their conventional tractors to drive, gave us two days home per week instead of one day, erased my accident record (fuel pump in Montana) so I got my penny per hour raise when Shelley got hers, and paid us for 4,200 miles per week even if we actually drove much less. Our scheduler "forgot to mention" that the dedicated pay rate is one cent less per mile than running the system, but when we found out about that, it was six weeks too late to change our minds, and $42/week for a few weeks isn't a big deal anyway. And for us, the conventional condo style tractor attached to the dedicated account was worth much more than a penny.

So here's how our lives changed: every minute from early Monday morning until sometime Friday or Saturday we were scheduled to pickup or deliver ASAP. The folks at Toro planned a two-day round trip for us, and then planned another round trip before the first was completed. Strange as it may seem, although we were guaranteed a minimum payment for 4200 miles/week and had no self-serving incentive to rush our lives, we felt lots of pressure to meet expectations. We found ourselves skipping meals, skipping daily showers, skipping our midnight quiet hours, too busy or tired to phone home and just driving, driving, driving all the time. Last week I went from Sunday to Thursday between showers. When Shelley went into a truck stop for a shower, I preferred to just sleep another thirty minutes, or fuel and service the truck so we could get going again as soon as she returned. It was crazy, it was exhausting, but it was self-inflicted; go figure.

Anyway, yesterday we delivered our last Toro load and went back on the system. The difference was immediate. We napped for three hours in Baraboo waiting for Schneider to assign a new load. We went from there to Neenah to pick up a loaded trailer from Kimberly Clark but when we got there, the load had been taken by some other team. After another hour's nap we received a new assignment to take a load from Oshkosh to Little Rock, but the delivery deadline was generous, so we stopped for a shower that afternoon and stopped again to sleep three hours that night. And our next load had an extra twenty-four hours available so we scheduled our tractor for a long overdue overhaul at the Memphis maintenance facility, checked into a motel, and have time now for email, restaurant meals, eight consecutive hours sleep, long showers, etc. We don't get paid to lie around like this, but the life style suits us better.

System loads will send us coast to coast again, something we look forward to. It will also mean going home less often. We'll probably be home only a two-day weekend every two weeks. Just think of the million truck drivers with wives and children at home!

That's the reality about truck driving, whether as a team or solo. The hours are brutal. A typical driver or team gets to go home one day per week, or two days per two weeks, or three days per three weeks out. Other than that, he's out one hundred percent of the time, sometimes so far away that even in an emergency, it could take three days to drive home. On top of that, when we were driving, the legal, federally-mandated maximum work day was fifteen hours per day but with creative bookkeeping, most solo drivers exceeded that. Team drivers divided the work in half, so they can "only" work twelve hours per day each. Although hours of service rules have recently changed, it's hard to think of another profession with hours that tough.

Getting drivers home regularly separates good companies from bad ones. The CB hissed with complaints about dispatchers keeping drivers on the road for weeks and weeks. Tough on family, tough on drivers. We had each other, but even teams want to get home.

For a company with as many drivers as Schneider to simultaneously manage time at home (TAH) and on-time load delivery, it becomes a logistical maze. Their logistics operation is one of the best in the industry. That didn't mean everyone got home every time they asked; people missed birthday parties and anniversaries, but generally the system to get people home worked. Not once in three years did we miss an event we'd arranged with the scheduler in advance.

By running the system (instead of having a dedicated account), we lived in the truck for an agreed-upon period, usually one to three weeks. That kept us and equipment busy and efficient. For most people, two or three weeks out is typical, and then they're ready for TAH. But, every team is different. We'd heard about a team, for instance, who sold their house, put their furniture in storage, and lived in the truck for months at a time. When they needed four walls and indoor plumbing, they stayed with their parents for a weekend. Saved money for sure, and they'd been doing it for several years.

Our arrangement was more typical. Toward the end of the driving period, Schneider would find and assign a trip that ended near or passed close to Madison. After delivery, we either bobtailed to our car which we'd previously parked at a Schneider-approved fuel stop, or we'd pick up the next load, park it at the fuel stop, and it would sit there during the time we were home, waiting for our return. Then we headed home.

Perfect timing wasn't absolutely guaranteed. TAH could be scheduled for Saturday and Sunday but might be a day in either direction. An important survival skill is staying good-humored when you arrive home an hour after the party's over.

One day at home per week is the gold standard of the long haul trucking industry. One day was never enough. As a matter of fact, it was unacceptable. So we'd often work it out with our STL to keep us out three weeks so we'd have a three-day weekend at home. Current competition and driver shortage has created many job offers with more options such as two days per week or three days for two weeks.

During our last year with Schneider, we joined their innovative "Home Run" program. For Home Run to work, three teams share two trucks. They agree to park the truck at one convenient, central location at the end of their two-week driving period, ready to be picked up right away – usually within hours -- by another team. With three teams and two trucks, while two teams are on the road, the third is at home for a full week. As far as the trucks are concerned, they don't get time off. The weeks are planned to begin and end on a Wednesday so weekend plans are never upset by the unpredictability of TAH dispatching.

It's like musical chairs, and it works like this. When Team One finishes a trip in Truck One, they unload their belongings, and Team Three, with their belongings, gets in and drives. Meanwhile, Team Two is still out driving Truck Two and has another week to go. Team One takes its week off, then meets Team Two at the parking spot and takes over Truck Two. This is not the truck they were previously driving, so they have to load their belongings into Truck Two. Team Three has just finished their first week. Another week goes by and Team Three finishes their second week, hands Truck One to

Team Two who have just finished their week at home, and so it goes. The tricky part is that everyone has to live reasonably close to the same central truck parking location.

With this program, everyone knows their schedule for the entire year in advance. Two weeks on, one off, which added up to seventeen weeks home each year. And recently, because of an even more severe driver shortage, we understand some teams are home for three weeks, on the road for three weeks! Who has time-off like that?

With a little inter-team cooperation, it's possible to stretch or shrink a trip here or there to accommodate anniversaries, weddings, special occasions. We shared basic truck equipment like broom, vacuum cleaner, carton of engine fluids, king pin hook, spare headlights and tail lights so we didn't have to move those things every trip, just left them in the truck. All of us developed well-organized, expedited cab-loading and unpacking systems.

In this program, you forfeit maximum annual pay, but the extra time-off suited us, and our other two teams, all non-smokers, shared the same emphasis on timeliness, cleanliness, and maintenance. For us it was perfect, and once we were part of the program, there was no going back to the old routine.

Whether it was a day or a week at home, it was tempting to cram too much into those precious hours. Besides laundry, bill paying, house and car maintenance, haircuts, and shopping, there was suddenly television, meals to cook, friends to visit. Whatever sleep/wake schedule we aimed for in the truck got turned on its head during time at home. After all, you both want to be awake for the movie you've waited a month to see.

Probably the hardest thing about team driving for us was figuring out how not to be tired all the time. Most team drivers – we were an exception – never stopped the truck to sleep. They had a driving pattern and stuck to it. One drove while one slept. One of our home run teams actually kept the same pattern during their time at home as they did on the road. She was the designated night driver, and at home while her husband slept,

Teri stayed up all night reading a book or watching a movie so she didn't have to readjust her clock six nights later. She's been doing that kind of time management for eight years. We never learned how.

The easiest thing about truck driving is that, once you've learned how, it's simple. Although at times it may be endless, hard, tiring, and demeaning, there is seldom more than one thing to think about at a time. If you're reasonably rested, tooling down the open road is great R&R for the mind. Anyone coming from complicated, overwhelming office work will find it's a straightforward assignment to drive a truck successfully, get to the destination efficiently, on time, safely. Schneider made all the tools for good trip planning available: fuel stop locations, suggested routes, good directions to facilities.

Despite its being simple, trucking came with built-in surprises, regular antidotes to numbing routine that spoils other jobs. Each new assignment was like a dice throw on a board game, letting you advance ten jumps this time, two the next, six on the turn after that. A new city, a new state, a new route, a new industry all added up to different versions of the game played on four seasonal game boards. Like kids, we both jumped on the computer when it beeped, our signal a new assignment had arrived. We never tired of that. Even if we'd been to the same destination ten times before, there was usually a new way to get there, or a new place to have a meal, or some sight on the way that we'd missed before but had time for on this trip.

As compensation for sometimes brutal and demeaning working conditions, there was the advantage of being in an industry that desperately needed drivers. That gave drivers the leverage of quitting and, if their driving record was good, being hired right back either by the same company or another. Owner-operators, of course, always had freedom and flexibility to put their truck and business in or out of commission whenever they felt like it. We exercised that option ourselves in the middle of our second year because we'd sold our house and had a busy remodeling project in the new one.

Schneider had absolutely no problem with a leave of absence and granted our request. Remodeling continued past Thanksgiving, but it was Schneider policy to welcome drivers back with no loss of seniority if they returned within six months of departure. Our group medical insurance coverage continued under COBRA laws. Schneider was so worried we wouldn't come back, in fact, they kept sending recruitment brochures in the mail and finally made the ultimate offer we couldn't refuse, a chance to be in the Home Run program mentioned before. We joined two other, hand-picked non-smoking teams in a brand new orange truck with just 748 odometer miles.

12

O ur two companion teams in the Home Run program were smart, veteran drivers with more than forty years' combined over-the-road experience. At the opposite end, we were newbies with lots to learn.

Many eyes follow a driver's performance. Shippers, consignees, DOT weigh stations, the highway patrol, everywhere somebody is looking. Within the company, people in customer service, maintenance, and operations watch you and the truck twenty-four hours a day. They control the overall picture, but within the truck and on the road, how you manage hour to hour is pretty much your own business. You are your own CEO.

We started managing our environment by fine-tuning the truck. Here's a list of our customizations:

- Installed dual CB antennas
- Replaced the cheap Schneider CB with an upgrade with longer range
- Installed a removable remote controlled stereo radio/cassette deck so we could keep our eyes on the road, not on the dial
- Screwed coat hooks to the walls, at least 4 double hooks

- Installed a digital outside air temperature thermometer on the dash (later became original equipment)
- Ran cable from a roof top cell phone antenna through the door jam to the dash
- Screwed a cell phone holder to the dash
- Stuck a compass to the dash with double-stick tape
- Stuck a digital clock on the dash
- Stuck a 2" x 3" monthly calendar to the dash
- Filled the coat closet with modular stacking plastic storage bins (for food)
- Screwed a map case to the right side of driver's seat
- Put in thick pile floor mats
- Bought a 12-volt vacuum cleaner
- Installed two hanging baskets
- Installed hanging paper towel roll
- Stocked kingpin lock, kingpin release handle extension hook, and jumper cables
- Furnished rags and gloves
- Furnished caulking gun with silicone caulk (for trailer leaks)
- Furnished crowbar, claw hammer, 2-pound sledge hammer
- Furnished push broom, whisk broom and dust pan

We hauled personal gear to and from the truck with every team switch:

- Schneider driver's handbook and trip planner
- Extra log books and blank forms like bills of lading and customs declarations
- Atlas (spiral-bound so it would open flat)
- Carton of state maps, truck stop guide and exit guides
- Pre-trip inspection checklist, laminated for durability
- Pocket calculator
- Walkman
- Hand-held single-channel CB radio
- 12-volt lunch-box type food warmer
- Two 12 volt refrigerators
- Cell phone
- Computer
- Laundry bag
- Two duffels for clean clothes
- Two small duffels with toilet kits, shower clogs, hand towels
- Mattress cover
- Bed sheets, pillow cases, comforter
- Pillows and blankets (down sleeping bags in winter)

- Food and drink
- Brief case with pens, pencils, envelopes, credit cards
- Clean throw rugs for the sleeper berth floor
- Books-on-tape (about 10)
- Binoculars
- Sunglass holders
- Flashlights
- Spare batteries
- Blizzard boots, coveralls and gloves
- Plastic milk crate full of engine fluids, WD-40
- Rubber gloves for fueling
- Big tackle box tool kit (This was David's personal collection of screwdrivers, pliers, wrenches, nuts, bolts and screws for minor repairs all over the truck. Also, electrical repair tools like fuses, continuity tester, wire strippers, terminals, terminal crimpers, wire nuts, tape.
- Small spare parts in the tool kit included flare tube fittings for bypassing the fuel filter, tire valve stem caps and inserts, glad hand gaskets, bulbs for parking and brake lights, electrical wire, baling wire.)

We made sure these company-supplied items were always in the truck:

- Load straps
- Charged fire extinguisher
- Glad hand spares and parts
- Tire chains for snow and ice
- Carton of spare tail lights, side lights, headlights, parking lights, backup light
- Emergency parking flares and triangles
- Engine oil, de-icer, washer fluid, radiator antifreeze
- Fuel filter element
- Schneider orange duct tape (8 rolls)

Missing on the truck was a spare tire. When we had a flat, we'd limp to the nearest authorized garage to have it replaced, unless it was a front tire. Flat front tires, *steers*, stop the truck cold. If that happened — luckily it didn't — we'd have to call a wrecker.

Every team switch began with a grocery shopping spree, followed by packing and loading all that food and drink into the car the day before departure. Rather than using their family car, one of our teams bought a "beater" to shuttle everything between home and truck and then stay parked there until they returned. Our parking locations were well-monitored and secure, not just any old back alley where cars might be hijacked or vandalized. In northern climates, it's not uncommon to come home to the car buried in a snow bank, so we kept ours equipped with shovel and jumper cables in case it was dead after sitting idle for two or three weeks. Usually the truck stop requires that drivers have written permission to leave a car, and many require that the drivers sign a liability waver.

We learned the hard way that before loading the truck, check first to see if the engine starts. Seems obvious, but if the engine doesn't start, our deadline just got revised.

David wrote about just such a winter experience:

Subject: Starting the truck

One of the things I do every day is drain the fuel/water separator. In a quarter cup of fuel that runs out of the drain valve, there is a trace of dirt and water on the bottom of the cup. But I hate to toss it into the environment, so I tend to stop draining after most of the water is drained, and I don't keep draining and draining until no trace of water comes out the drain valve like you're supposed to. Last Tuesday morning when the Madison temperature was eight degrees below zero, this came back to haunt me.

We don't have any place to plug in the engine heater at our parking place when we're in Madison, so we took our chances last weekend and lost. It would not start. We called a local wrecker service on his busiest morning of the year and eventually he arrived. The expensive jump start worked for ten seconds until all the fuel in the injectors got used up. Then the whole truck had to be dragged by an even bigger wrecker to a warm garage for a few hours to thaw everything. This all took nine hours, so the day that started at dawn didn't really get rolling until 18:30.

Have we learned anything from all this? I guess! From now on we let the engine idle in cold weather, even if it's for several days. Schneider would have approved letting the engine idle at the truck stop for the entire three days we were home.

Even if the engine starts, there's no telling what mischief might have happened since someone was last in the truck, even if it was just hours ago, so we had to do the entire DOT pre-trip inspection checklist before starting a trip. If a tire went flat or vandals fiddled with something, you'd better know about it. If there was anything that might delay a pick-up or delivery, Schneider needed to know now. A good inspection took at least twenty minutes, a quick walk-around only five minutes. So while I loaded the truck, David did the pre-trip.

This can be the messiest part of the entire job, crawling around under a dripping trailer in wet weather in a muddy lot. And it can be the most frigid part. Our Boy Scout inventory had a wardrobe of good, tall, waterproof shoes, tough rubber gloves, and warm clothes. All that muddy stuff comes off and is stowed in the sidebox once the inspection is finished.

Naturally, we paid particular attention to all eighteen tires. At every fuel stop, toilet stop, pick-up and delivery, we thumped each one and listened for the telltale thud of a flat. Truck tires are not just big car tires. They have several more belts of reinforcing cords, are inflated to 100 psi, and are pricey. Because they travel so many miles in a year, the tread gets worn thin while the body is still young so they are re-treaded before reaching the end of useful life.

Part of every tire inspection was to check each one for nails, uneven wear, minimum legal tread depth (using a calibrated metal gauge), and for low tire pressure by thumping with a hammer or billy club. You can't tell just by looking because a flat often looks normal. But you can tell by thumping. After a little while the ear gets tuned, and it's easy to hear the flat's dull thud if a tire has 80 psi instead of 100.

We averaged a flat tire every week, sometimes five a week, mostly on trailers that had been sitting idle for awhile, dropped by drivers who didn't notice or take time to report a flat. Motivating a driver to look for maintenance to do on a trailer he's never going to see again rarely happens.

Changing a tire is not a do-it-yourself project. Dismounting and re-mounting the tire on a wheel takes a sledge hammer and a heavy duty power tool, and mounting the wheel on the truck takes a dozen large lug nuts hammered on with the biggest pneumatic impact wrench you've ever seen. Even standing around watching, we wore ear protection.

Although a truck may limp along with one soft tire in a cluster of four, the soft one will eventually self-destruct and throw rubber and belting all over the highway. Usually the first thing to fly off is the entire re-tread belt, called a "gator," big enough to cause serious damage to any vehicle — truck or car — if you run over it. When a gator comes flying off, it can take a fair amount of equipment along with it. Mud flaps and trailer brake hoses are especially vulnerable. In the roadway, loose mud flaps are deadly debris that can easily break a windshield.

They're so dangerous that drivers routinely report gators on the CB. "Heads up eastbound, you got a big old gator in the hammer lane, mile marker 2-0-1." East bound trucks start crowding into the slow lane well before the 2-0-1, getting lined up to miss the gator.

If a trailer brake hose gets ripped off by debris in the road, like a gator, the spring loaded fail-safe trailer brakes come on immediately. You sometimes see those four black streaks on the highway where a trailer suddenly locked up and skidded toward a place to park on the shoulder. Never happened to us, but it represents about $3200 worth of trailer tires with flat spots.

Front wheel tires are special. Maximum load for a drive tire in a tandem set is 4,250 pounds each. Maximum load on a steer is 6,000 pounds. Besides stopping the trip right now, a steer wheel blowout is dangerous. Because of this, the steer tires are extra good and extra expensive. We never experienced a flat or soft steer and very seldom even heard about one.

Before buckling seatbelts or moving the truck an inch, whether after TAH or after a change of drivers, we filled out the logbook, a tedious and perpetual routine. To start a trip, each driver's logbook is brought up to date showing "off duty" hours during time at home. We learned early not to let this task slide because trying to reconstruct driving history is like trying to remember all the moves in a chess game. It's not uncommon to pull into a weigh station parking area and see drivers filling out several pages of log book entries. Maybe they were cheating, but more likely they were just catching up.

Trip planning was so important to our over-all job satisfaction that even before leaving home, we'd call the office to see if our new assignment was ready so we could do some early scheming. Advance information might trigger ideas for a mini-adventure or a stop-over visit.

To make trip planning easier, we accumulated a small shelf of trip planning books. This was before computer-based mapping programs and GPS systems which must make trip-planning a piece of cake. We did it the old-fashioned way using the big Rand McNally truckers' atlas, individual state maps, interstate exit guide, United States interstate system map, truck stop guide, Schneider route planning guide. The truckers' atlas has all legal truck routes color coded, and it has special sections covering each state's unique limits on state highway load limits, height and width restrictions, wheel base limitations.

Unlike being in a car, pulling off any-old-place to check a map wasn't possible. We were on a trajectory, launched, with few, if any bail-outs. We clipped our route — a cheat-sheet written in black marker large enough to see highway numbers at a glance — right to the dash and kept a pocket flashlight next to it for nighttime reading. The cheat-sheet listed every road, the direction on that road, the mileage to the next road, and exit numbers where applicable. Some trips would have over twenty highway changes; others would be all on just one interstate.

It was a nightmare to miss a turn. Maps have roads, but they don't tell you where there's enough room to turn around. We'd have to wake the other person, scramble for the map, all the while looking for a place to stop or turn off. It was bound to delay the trip.

Messages from the satellite with every detail about the assignment were stored in the monitor. As we approached the consignee, one of us located that message with street directions and read them, turn by turn, to the driver. It wasn't uncommon to use binoculars to read street signs hundreds of yards away so that in a busy city, the driver had enough lead time to get in the correct lane. Missing a turn in a city is the absolute worst because there is no predicting what obstacles lurk left, lurk right, lurk ahead or surprise — lurk above in the form of low bridges or wires overhead.

One trip planning detail that couldn't be overlooked was bridge height. Long haul vans are built to a standard dimension of 13.5 feet tall and 8.5 feet wide. It's neither advisable nor possible to drive through a hole smaller than that. Many drivers learned the hard way that their route included a low bridge. As car drivers we never noticed the yellow diamond signs all over the place advising truckers of upcoming bridge heights, but now and ever since the first day on the road in Green Bay, we notice.

When we deliberately wandered off onto state highways — skinny roads — it was important to check the fine print in the back of the trucker's atlas to make sure there were no low bridges or size and weight restrictions. Once in Massachusetts we found ourselves stopped in the street looking up at a 12-foot railroad bridge. We were lucky that time. I got out of the truck, stood in the middle of the road, stopped traffic from both directions, and using the walkie-talkie talked David through a blind-side back into a convenience store parking lot. There's nothing like that to draw a crowd.

Another time on US-2 in Philadelphia we crept under a bridge marked 13'-3" because by the time we saw the sign, backing up was unthinkable. That time, I stood up on the passenger seat, leaned backward out the door window watching at eye-level whether the top of the trailer would be ripped to shreds. We had no excuse in that case because Pennsylvania has a special trucker's road map with all steep hills and low bridges well marked. We were lucky again, and pretty stupid.

When and where to buy fuel was a math problem, and since David likes math problems, he planned our fuel stops. Our truck had two 100 gallon tanks for diesel fuel. We typically averaged less than 1,000 miles per day with fuel consumption at 4.5 to 7.5 miles per gallon, depending on the weight of the load and headwind. So, unless fuel consumption was high, we never had to refuel more than once per day.

The whole trip pivots around fuel stops. "Fair" trip planning includes a stop when the tank's almost empty, then another stop to top up the tanks when it's time for a shower. "Good" planning includes timing the fuel stop for early morning when you want a hot shower. "Great" timing means getting to the fuel stop late at night while your partner sleeps. The driver refuels and parks in a quiet spot, does a good post trip inspection, logs himself off-duty, takes a shower, and sets the alarm before squeezing into the sleeper. When the alarm goes off, the partner gets up, takes his/her shower and heads down the road while the off-duty driver sleeps on. Every team does this differently, but this system worked for us.

Schneider gave us credit cards to use for charging diesel fuel. First choice was always to refuel at a clean and sparkly Schneider OC. To supplement company-owned OC's, Schneider published a state-by-state list of approved fuel stops where they'd negotiated favorable pricing and where the facilities were clean and efficient. There could be many truck stops on the route, but only one approved by Schneider. Almost none were on skinny roads. And if ever we got caught short of fuel at a non-approved stop, we had to call Schneider, tail between our legs, for permission to buy $50 worth of diesel.

Besides filling the tanks, we topped up all the fluids, added deicer to the diesel in winter, did a quick en route inspection — especially the tires — washed mud off headlights, tail lights, side lights and reflector tape, emptied trash and washed the windshield, side windows, and every single mirror. It was extra work to polish the windshield with Rain-Ex window wax every few days, but worth it. Bugs washed off easily, and rain blew off without impairing visibility.

Good truck stops have work platforms at each pump. They are very wide, stable ladders on wheels, essential for washing windows on a cab-over. Some truck stops also have water hoses for hosing the mud off the doors and windows and around the fuel filler caps. Although Schneider authorized regular truck washes, inevitably our tractor was dirty and these garden hoses used with a squeegee kept the doors, at least, clean.

There's another special thing about truck stops. It's one of the few places where the driver is king. Every truck pulling up to the pumps buys at least $200 worth of diesel fuel, so truck stop employees fall all over themselves to be courteous and helpful. We always got the free ice cream cone at Big Spring, Nebraska, free coffee refill (when you provide your own mug) almost everywhere, and of course, free showers. Truck stops competed with each other to supply the biggest, most luxurious Turkish towels and biggest pieces of apple pie.

Sometimes, in spite of the best trip planning, things fall apart. Sometimes information is outdated. Sometimes information is unclear. Sometimes you're too tired to notice. Directions to a specific location coming over the computer look something like this:

S35468 PETRO TS
12345 FRONTAGE ROAD
PORTAGE, WI
608-742-5858
WI I-94 WB EXIT #106. TL OVER
BRIDGE. 1ST SL TR. FTG RD
TR GO .5 MI ON L

Translated this means:

(ID S35468) Petro Truck Stop
12345 Frontage Road
Portage, Wisconsin
608-742-5858

Wisconsin I-94 (westbound), take exit number 106 and turn left to go over the bridge. At first stop light turn right. At frontage road turn right and go one-half mile to find destination on left hand side.

Note that these instructions are for westbound travelers. Traveling eastbound, we'd do the mental gymnastics ahead of time and jot these on our hand-written cheat sheet clipped to the dashboard. This saved us lots of headaches trying to think in reverse in rush-hour traffic in a monsoon.

To work well, good instructions must be updated whenever there are changes. Drivers are encouraged to report mistakes or corrections. There were always mistakes that needed corrections. Sometimes that happened and other times it didn't. Here's my account:

Subject: Lost in Chester, PA

We've been lost in Chester twice this year. Chester is a part of urban Philadelphia, sandwiched between I-95 and the Delaware River, just south of Eddystone, Pennsylvania, and about fifteen miles north of Wilmington, Delaware. Our customer here is the Kimberly-Clark factory, a paper company enjoying convenient riverside waste disposal. They make diapers - diapers for all ages - in two imposing plants built of gray concrete.

Normally, Schneider sends us street-by-street, turn-by-turn directions to each of our destinations. Normally, these directions get us to the door; sometimes, there is a typo or other mistake and we drivers are encouraged to send corrections via satellite. David and I are diligent about sending in corrections because we know from experience how terrifying it is to be lost, never knowing if you'll turn a corner and be on a dead-end, or face a low clearance bridge, or a no-trucks residential area, or a weight restricted county road, etc. So, our directions to Kimberly-Clark arrived, sending us north on I-95.

Two days earlier, construction on I-95 made our directions to Kimberly-Clark obsolete. A neon orange detour sign pointed us off the interstate into Chester proper. We followed. There is no such thing as Chester, proper. Chester is as far from proper as Calcutta is from Paris. Chester is one of those places people like us don't visit, ever. Chester is one of those places featured on "Cops." The Methodist Church on the corner is riddled with holes, right through the stained glass windows. Razor wire loops through fences to keep people out of vacant lots. Whole rows of row houses are bulldozed, and the few left standing in mid-block spew out their Goodwill sofas and rotted mattresses, broken chairs and bottles, right down the moldy staircase, out the landing and onto the sidewalk. Packs of skinny dogs circle in the middle of the street and nobody is anywhere.

And we were getting lost. The neon detour signs disappeared and we were getting deeper and deeper into Chester. At street end we spotted a Dollar Store. The windows were boarded, but a couple of baggy-panted hip-hopping youths were in the parking lot, a parking lot which looked big enough for our huge truck to turn into and back out of, and which had a telephone booth. So David departed the truck and strode past the hoppers to the phone to call Kimberly-Clark for further directions. I locked the doors.

Our instructions were to retrace our steps, turn left toward the river and proceed to the plant. So we retraced our steps, turned left and found ourselves facing the entrance to a naval shipyard, not a paper plant as promised. A small church on our right with a parishioner's parking lot gave us just enough room to squeeze into and back out of. But before leaving, David checked with the guard at the shipyard entrance to inquire about the whereabouts of the huge Kimberly-Clark factory on the Delaware River. The guard pointed north.

So we went north on what must have been Main Street. Every couple of blocks a relic row house still stood, neighbor-less, complete with whitewashed stoop and hanging plastic pot of red geraniums. Now, these were little residential miracles, I thought. Who had the guts to stay in Chester, anyway? I guessed some strong matriarch, arms folded when the bulldozers came and dozed her neighbors under, standing firm, defying the Urban Planning Commission, paying her taxes, and keeping that geranium alive.

Main Street had a couple more churches, a bar, a pawn shop with razor wire. On the corner sat a two-story brick structure with a huge, bronze plaque which read, "William Penn 1682 - Essex House. When Penn landed here, he stayed in this Inn." The side of the building was caved in, bricks tumbling into a weed patch where the lobby must have been. Around the corner another Pennsylvania Historical Commission plaque proclaimed the location of Martin Luther King's first church. The lot was vacant; actually the whole square block was vacant, just that sign on a stick by the curb. The history of Chester has become one vacant lot after another.

But across the street was Kimberly-Clark. We were found. So when people ask us what we like about trucking, this is the kind of story I like to tell them. Not that there was much to like about being lost in Chester. It's not something I'd choose to do. But it was an experience I'm grateful to have had. I know more about this country.

I'm glad I was in a big tough truck and not a little car. I'm glad I don't have to live in Chester (or East St. Louis, or Compton, or parts of New Orleans or Miami or Los Angeles or Detroit or Chicago where we've been).

I feel mighty sorry for the people who do.

13

Load assignments and the trips they represent are not created equal. Sometimes our first words when we read the new assignment were "Oh shit, it's a live load," or "Thank god, it's a drop and hook." If the assignment was a "live" load, we had to back an empty trailer to the loading dock and then wait for the shipper, when he got around to it, to load the goods into the trailer. Live unload was the same, waiting for the consignee, when he got around to it, to unload at the destination. Obviously, being paid by the mile, waiting for anything was costly and even though Schneider compensated us if the delay was excessive, it didn't amount to the same as if we'd been driving down the road.

To make the best of this down time, one of us would trip plan. The other would nap. But try taking a nap with a forklift, sometimes two forklifts, rumbling up and down 53' of trailer floor for an hour or more. It isn't easy. Not only that, you're always on alert for the forklift operator to bang on the door, hand you the bill of lading, and tell you to pull away from the dock to make room for the next load.

Occasionally the dock crew would ask us how we wanted the trailer loaded. Heavy stuff like printing paper or canned tomatoes can be loaded nose-heavy, tailgate-heavy, or balanced. We always asked for just a little nose-heavy so we could slide the trailer tandem axles all the way forward. That shorter wheelbase made it easier to make the turn at a sharp corner. Some drivers preferred the tandems as far back as state bridge laws allow because they thought more weight on the tractor springs made a smoother ride. When it came to a very slightly bouncier ride versus clipping a stoplight, we chose the rougher ride.

Sometimes we had an assignment where we had to unload the trailer onto the consignee's warehouse floor using a manual hydraulic pallet jack on wheels. Schneider paid an extra $80 for a "driver-unload" and if it was a quick unload, $80 seemed worth it. But nothing was quick at a grocery distributor where many different products are all mixed up on pallets for efficient shipping, not necessarily efficient unloading. We had to re-stack each pallet by product according to a little printed schematic the distributor handed us. Each warehouse had their own unique scheme for how high and wide a stack of cartons could be on each pallet.

Doing a live unload was one of the few times we were an integral part of the busy dock community instead of just being onlookers. Unloading became a trucker's social event spanning across fifteen dock doors, a trucker at each one struggling with his mountain of cartons. It was a rare opportunity for physical exercise, so we actually enjoyed the experience. One time Walgreen's let us keep a huge box of candy canes that had been mistakenly shipped in excess, just in time for Christmas. I think we had them for two years.

On the other hand, "drop and hook" loads were already loaded and waiting to be picked up. The ultimate assignment, theoretically, is when the drop and the hook both take place at the same facility. You take in a load, drop it and drive a hundred yards to the new load, hook it up, and scram. Sometimes, though, the assignment required dropping a trailer at one location, then driving to a second location for the new load. Time spent going around in circles, finding the second drop yard, tracking down a particular trailer with a certain number in a lot full of dirty trailers is time donated to the company at no pay. No miles, no pay.

Drop and hooks, theoretically the best assignments, could end up being the worst if an empty trailer exchange was involved. If an assignment said, "Pick up empty trailer #12345 and drop at . . . ." we could find ourselves on a series of wild goose chases, trying to find trailer #12345 in a place where Schneider thought it was parked. But it wasn't there. Maybe lots of other empty trailers were there, but not #12345. Or maybe no empty trailers were there and we'd have to send a message asking where to go to find one. Sometimes we went to four or five different locations looking for an empty. If this happened in Los Angeles, as it often did, we were ready to steal an empty trailer rather than go to another drop lot to find it. And sometimes that's what we did.

The lost empty trailer situation was so bad that Schneider offered rewards to drivers if they spotted one hiding behind an abandoned gas station or in somebody's farm yard. It was like being a cop looking for the criminal's license plate as you drove down the road; we weren't good cops and never found one. But dozens of lost trailer numbers appeared every week on the satellite monitor, so the problem was huge. By now, GPS tracking systems may have solved that.

Eventually, the load was ready and so were we. Accompanying every load is an essential piece of paperwork called the bill of lading. That is the invoice, or receipt, for the shipping service. The bill is generated by the shipper and given to the driver, who signs it, when the load is picked up. It lists the origin of the shipment, goods in the load, weight, hazardous materials, and destination. The driver absolutely must have a bill of lading for each load. In an emergency, if it happens to be lost, he can write up his own using his pad of blank bill of lading forms.

Bills of lading are checked routinely at Ports of Entry located in western and southwestern states like Wyoming, Montana, Arizona, California. They are special types of weigh stations located at the state line and unlike typical weigh stations, they are always open, and some require that you show them your bill of lading. If you are stopped by law enforcement, all paperwork including bill of lading, log books, driver's license, vehicle registration, medical certificate have to be produced.

I remember my first time being stopped by a State Trooper like it was ten minutes ago. We'd come into Wyoming from the south on a skinny road and I'd gone through an out-of-the-way Port of Entry. When we got onto the interstate going east, we passed another Port of Entry with a big sign, "All Vehicles Must Enter." I reasoned that I'd already been through Wyoming's Port of Entry and whizzed on by. Within seconds, a State Trooper was flashing Christmas tree lights behind me and, heart thundering, I pulled over. I got out of the truck and met him half way. He was motioning like mad for me to back up towards the truck. (Later I learned the Trooper approaches you, not the reverse.)

"Bring me all your paperwork," he growled.

Shaking, I turned back to get it and David poked his head out to see what trouble I'd gotten us into. I found both our logbooks, bills of lading, and walked back to the flashing bear. I nestled in beside his shotgun and summoned the courage to ask if I was supposed to stop at the second Port of Entry east of Cheyenne since I'd already cleared one south of Cheyenne. He didn't look up, just kept thumbing through the logbooks. He typed something into his onboard computer.

Finally he said, "Nope."

I assumed he was answering my original question.

He handed me paperwork and said, "Thanks, you're all set."

Moral of the story is to keep legal logbooks. It buys great peace of mind.

If the load was a drop and hook, the bill of lading was stuck in a little aluminum envelope called the nose box on the front face of the trailer. Sometimes, the nose box was sealed with a tamper-proof plastic tie so vandals couldn't read the bill of lading and know what the load contained. After all, drop lots are generally in low-rent, rundown parts of town where vandals have easy access to trailers.

In our briefcase, we accumulated a collection of forms for generating documentation and reports. Bill of lading blanks, Schneider delivery reports, expense reports for reimbursement, envelopes, tally sheets, blank logbooks, Canada customs forms, US Customs forms.

Going into Canada the first time was one of those experiences that makes travel within the states seem like a cakewalk. Crossing the northern border probably isn't much different than crossing into China. They're both foreign countries. They're often manned by uniformed people acting out their officialdom. Filling out customs forms, finding the broker's office and the customs office, learning the protocol in a foreign country was good practice at figuring out new routines. Even though many of these details are spelled out in the Schneider manual, doing it the first time is a challenge and after you're through the gate, you feel some pride and a sense of accomplishment. Plus you're glad it's over, at least for that border. Every border entry is different, even into the same country, laid out in a novel way and you have to hunt for the path through the maze -- hauling a 53' trailer. Just ask David.

Subject: One Way

"One way" refers to USA/Canada border customs procedures. There is one and only one way to correctly proceed. Get it wrong and you can get stuck for hours straightening it out. Last night we approached the border crossing at Port Huron,

Michigan, fearing both "one way" hazards. We had a full truckload of Scripto cigarette lighters from Mexico. They had been sealed "in bond" entering the United States, and we had to get U.S. customs to stamp our paperwork confirming the load was still unopened before we could legally depart the United States. Problem is, normal traffic does not stop at U.S. customs *departing* the United States. You must go through U.S. customs *returning* to the United States, but going the other way, you just sail on past. How can you even find U.S. customs on departure? Shelley was madly searching the "Canada" section of our reference guide that was supposed to tell us everything about this complicated procedure. Nada.

It was after dark. A light rain was making everything too dark or too bright. We followed the signs "TO CANADA." It was like poking my nose into a blind alley. Can't stop in the middle of the highway. Have to keep moving, but where is Customs? The road is six lanes wide; which side is the parking lot for Customs? Suddenly there appeared the row of toll booths just before the big bridge over the St. Claire River. Talk about a one way street! Once I got up close to a toll booth with traffic piling up behind me, it would be all over. Two choices at that point: block traffic for as long as it takes to clear a bond; or cross the bridge into Canada, explain it all to Canadian Customs, U-turn and come right back, clear U.S. customs, U-turn again, pay the $12 toll again, cross the river a third time and clear Canadian Customs.

In desperation I called on the CB, "Hey, where's U.S. Customs heading eastbound?" and slowed to a crawl hoping I'd get an answer before I got trapped in the toll booth.

Immediately, I was rescued by the truck right behind me.

"That you Schneider? Pull over and stop right there. You park along the wall in the right hand lane and walk across the road. That's U.S. Customs on your left."

Incredulous, I stopped in the right-hand lane about six truck lengths short of the toll booth, grabbed the paperwork and wove through five busy lanes of traffic in the rain, found the door to U.S. Customs, got the forms stamped (he didn't want to see the seals on the trailer doors), re-crossed the freeway and continued across, free and clear. Simple.

And then we headed for the drop lot. Drop lots, as the name implies, are places where trailers — empty and loaded — are dropped awaiting either delivery, loading, or unloading. These lots are generally unsupervised vacant lots on cheap real estate, although some have complicated automated security gates for which the driver is given instructions ahead of time. Codes to open gates come over the satellite with the assignment.

Some drop lots, particularly where there is a heavy concentration of hijack activity like California, New York, Chicago, have a guard shack for checking in and out. These lots are operated by the company, surrounded by tall, chain link fences topped with razor wire. Instructions for what to do at the guard shack vary. Some post notices on the shack window warning drivers to stay in the truck. Others allow only one driver in the shack at a time. Some guards only talk on the CB. Expect to make mistakes the first time at a new guard shack; it's one of the hazards of driving no one ever told us about.

Where there is no guard shack, dark nights are scary times to be crawling around between trailers in a desolate drop lot. We felt better when there was high security.

Rail yards, where truck meets train, are the most heavily-supervised and security-minded places. No tourist gets inside a rail yard. Usually tucked in the center of the city and hard-to-find, they're busy, noisy, and like something out of a 1940's movie. When we were lucky, we'd get to watch the giant walking gantry crane lift our trailer off the rail car and lower it to the ground next to the truck. Or we'd loop through row after row of trailers, scanning numbers to find ours somewhere among them, dodging slow-moving train engines and fast moving yard jockeys along the way.

When you pick up a trailer from a rail yard, you and a company guard walk around the trailer and fill out a special damage report form. Railroad equipment is rough on equipment, poking lots of holes in trailers and breaking and bending landing gear. Claims between truck and rail companies over who did what to which trailer keeps company lawyers busy. The railroad files a condition report when the trucking company delivers a trailer to the rail yard at the beginning of the rail trip. The driver's report documents its condition at the other end of the trip, a lot like the damage sheet when you rent a car.

After finding the trailer at a drop lot, rail yard, or shipper, you need to couple it to the tractor. The two are connected by a short, fat, steel "king pin" under the front of the trailer. It slides into and locks in place in the "fifth wheel," the big greasy horseshoe mechanism on the back of every tractor. Trailer height and tractor height must match closely for this mechanism to catch properly. A trailer that's too low will just bang into the back of the tractor and might cause damage. A trailer that's too high will pass above the fifth wheel jaws or, worse yet, get jammed with the king pin partially stuck in the top part of the locking mechanism. This is an accident waiting to happen. Undetected, it can lead to de-coupling on the highway, one of a driver's worst nightmares.

Schneider teaches the proper technique which is to back the tractor close to the nose of the trailer, get out of the cab and go back to see how things line up. When both of us were awake, to make things go quickly, one of us would stand eye-level with the mechanism, signaling the driver when/if things were aligned. The king pin had to be aligned left/right to enter the slot in the fifth wheel, and the leading edge of the trailer had to be just high enough to contact the sloped ramp of the very greasy fifth wheel platform. If necessary, the nose of the trailer could be cranked up or down by a hand crank which was part of the landing gear, or telescoping legs, on the front end of a trailer.

Assured that the trailer and tractor are aligned, the driver backs up slowly but powerfully, driving the fifth wheel platform under the trailer nose until the king pin stops the tractor dead in its tracks with a big bang and a jolt. At that point the powerful fifth wheel jaw mechanism has automatically snapped shut on the king pin and securely locked it to the tractor. A mandatory tug test in low gear makes sure the trailer won't pull off and go rolling all by itself down the road.

In snow, mud or loose gravel, the tractor drives might spin and fail to slide back under the trailer. Then it's time to engage the "power divider," an electrical 4-wheel drive clutch that separates the forward drive axle from the rear axle. With the power divider switch up, both axles have power, instead of just the forward axle.

David's trainer taught him what to do when the fifth wheel plate had just been slathered with a fresh coat of lubrication grease. Spread on a half inch thick, unless you're careful, it would be plowed right off onto the leading edge of the trailer where it would lubricate nothing but our clothes. So instead, we liked to crank the trailer up a little too high, then back the tractor under the nose almost to the king pin, then crank the trailer down gently onto that nice fresh bed of grease before locking onto the pin.

Standing on the back catwalk deck of the tractor, it was my job to connect the electrical plug for trailer lights and join two sets of "glad hand" assemblies, which resemble radiator caps screwed together. One assembly was for the trailer service brake air hose and the other for the parking brake air hose.

Finally we cranked up the landing gear. Landing gear telescopes up and down to adjust the trailer nose height for coupling and uncoupling, and it must be cranked all the way up while driving so it doesn't get torn off. You know you've forgotten to crank it up when you hear it scrape and grind against the pavement. It happens. You just hope no one's watching.

There's a big difference between cranking up an empty trailer and one that's fully loaded with 25,000 pounds in the nose. The jack-screws in the landing gear legs are driven by a two-speed gear box. Cranking clockwise or counter clockwise runs the legs up or down; shoving the crankshaft in or out shifts to high or low gear. Trailers from different manufacturers come in every permutation of clockwise/counter-clockwise, in/out gear operation. Each one had to be figured out by trial and error.

Plus, landing gear and crank handles stick out where they are vulnerable and almost all are damaged to some extent after a year of use. Damage does not make them easier to crank. Even in low gear, cranking a loaded trailer very far up or down can be a real workout, especially when it takes forty turns on the crank to make the adjustment. It's good exercise, and for that reason we didn't mind it unless the trailer was squeezed tight next to another and there was no room to stand. Sometimes we'd find ourselves actually crouched beneath the neighboring, grease-covered trailer, trying to crank our trailer's landing gear. Handy hiding place if it happened to be raining.

The reverse process, uncoupling, goes quickly because there's no tractor-trailer alignment to do. First, the electrical plug and glad hands for both air hoses are disconnected from the trailer and hung up neatly on the tractor's back wall. It's tempting to just drop the disconnected lines on the catwalk especially if the next trailer will be hooked up in a few minutes, but there is the unpleasant possibility they will drop down and wrap around the drive shaft.

The landing gear is cranked down just far enough to lift up the trailer's nose to take some weight off the tractor's fifth wheel. If for some reason the footpads on the landing gear are missing, you need to find something like a flat rock or scrap of wood to put under them regardless of whether you're dropping in a dirt or asphalt lot. Otherwise, the sharp edges of the landing gear can cut through the ground, eventually tipping the nose down and making it impossibly low for a tractor to get under it. There were places in the West Sacramento drop yard where landing gear, even with footpads, punched holes a foot deep into the blacktop parking surface. Some fancy drop lots have a concrete strip for the landing gear so the driver has to make sure he parks with the trailer positioned just so.

You can tell when to stop cranking. When enough weight comes off the tractor, you hear a hissing sound as the automatic leveling valve near the tractor axle dumps air from the tandem air springs. Then a good hard yank pulls the fifth-wheel release handle out to the unlocked position so the tractor can be slowly pulled out from under. (Pulling the handle was something Bobbie back in Green Bay could never do.) You pull away slowly, so if the landing gear collapses or sinks into the ground, the trailer will only drop onto the tractor frame, not all the way down on its nose.

We always used a long extension handle, or fifth-wheel puller, to hook onto the release handle. This let us avoid ducking under the greasy end of a trailer, groping for the release handle. With practice, you learn to slap the puller upward against the release handle and in the same mighty yank, pull perpendicularly toward yourself.

Pulling the release handle for the fifth wheel is child's play compared to pulling the retractable pin on the trailer tandems. The whole process of sliding tandems was designed to discourage anyone from being a truck driver, especially a solo driver. As mentioned in a previous chapter, the reason trailer tandems slide is so weight on each truck axle doesn't exceed the maximum allowed on state and federal highways. State DOT scales, known to truckers as "chicken coops" or just plain "coops," randomly weigh trucks anytime night or day. Some drivers go miles out of their way to bypass open coops. Those trucks are overweight, and the fines for being overweight are significant, depending on how overweight you are and which state you're in. Some bypasses in the western states are so popular that the state has moveable scales they can haul in and catch you trying to cheat.

Federal law says total truck weight cannot exceed 80,000 pounds (unless you have a special "overweight" permit) and within that total, tractor steers (front wheels) cannot exceed 12,000 pounds total, and tractor drives (positioned under the front part of the trailer) or trailer tandems (under rear of trailer) cannot exceed 34,000 pounds per set of eight wheels.

The only way you know if the weights are right is by weighing each of the three axle groupings on a truck scale. It's guesswork until then. When you do know how much weight has to be shifted off one end or the other, there's some simple math to figure how many holes the trailer tandems have to be moved on the slide rails.

David was the mathematician on this detail also. The math is simple but he still managed to apply the correction in the wrong direction one time and had to pay Georgia $15 for being 1,500 pounds too heavy on the trailer wheels. We shifted the tandems back the other way right there at the chicken coop and went across the scales again before getting permission to continue on down Georgia's highways.

The other reason to shift the trailer tandems is because of different wheel base dimensions allowed on various state highways. The wheel base limitations are referred to as the bridge rule. Most states had no bridge rule restrictions that affected us, but about a dozen had their little hoops we had to jump through. If we pulled a trailer on a state highway in Indiana, for example, there was a place marked on all Schneider trailers showing where the driver had to set the trailer tandems to be legal on Indiana state highways.

To accommodate requirements of all kinds, trailer axles sit on a sliding carriage (rails) with a lot of holes spaced a few inches apart. A large, retractable pin secures the sliding part to the rails when they are aligned at the right place for proper weight distribution between the front and back of the trailer. The principle is the same as a teeter-totter where you change the pivot point to give the lighter kid equal leverage.

Sliding the trailer tandems was something we practiced for fifteen minutes in school just once and never with our training engineers. And it ain't easy, especially for a solo driver who has to jump in and out of the cab several times to get it right. There were many times when we'd watch a solo driver going berserk trying to do this alone, so David would go offer a hand.

After a lot of frustrating trial and error, the procedure David and I developed was for me to drive and for him to stand next to the back trailer wheels. He always used the fifth wheel puller because he could get two hands on it, plus he didn't have to reach under the trailer where his head would be mere inches from the tires.

First thing is to make sure the trailer brakes are locked (so its tandems can't move) and the tractor brakes are off (so the tractor can move). Watching David in the mirror while he yanked with all his might on the handle of the pin retraction mechanism, I'd jog back and forth until the pin broke loose and caught in the unlocked position detent. Then, by inching forward or backward depending on David's hand signals, the pin would line up with the proper hole (3" either way is too much), and David would slap the handle off its detent. Usually he'd catch the hole on the fly and the spring-loaded mechanism drove the pin into the hole.

But sometimes the pin was just plain stuck and David couldn't pull hard enough on the handle to break it free. When that happened I'd set the parking brakes, get down and go back to pull on the extension handle while David beat on the pin with our special two pound hammer, packed just for this kind of special job.

And there were times the slider and rails were so corroded they wouldn't slide anyway, so then the engine had to be gunned to break loose everything and whoops – we'd slide miles past the right hole. Or sometimes, especially on gravel, nothing breaks the rusty mechanism loose and the trailer, in spite of locked brakes, moves anyway, eight trailer tires skidding across the gravel. Then we'd scour the lot looking for boulders or lumber or chocks to wedge under the trailer wheels like doorstops to keep all those wheels from skidding. We did that a few times before realizing we could drive pretty far before being checked by DOT for proper wheel base or load balance, far enough to get off the gravel and onto a dry, paved surface with plenty of friction.

In addition to sticky rails, van trailers come with a variety of problems. They can leak, be dirty, pilfered, loaded improperly, and not fit the loading dock. The trailers we hauled have big double doors in back. There's a flimsy hook and chain on each side to hold the doors open against the trailer side walls. If these are broken or missing, chances are the doors will get sprung by swinging open against the neighboring trailers while rolling in or out of a slot. We used our same special two-pound sledge hammer to help close the locks on sprung doors.

To prove that a trailer went from shipper to destination without being opened and pilfered, the doors are double-sealed with a padlock and a plastic wire tie. If a customer receives a load with things missing, the driver has to be able to show that while it was in his possession, the doors stayed shut. Schneider used big orange plastic wire ties with a unique serial number on each one to slip with the padlock through the latch. It was not very useful unless you remembered to ask the shipper to initial the serial number on the bill of lading, showing that he witnessed that exact seal on the doors. A broken or missing seal meant someone had opened the doors during the trip. You don't want them thinking it's you.

Some shippers applied their own seals to the doors. They used simple plastic or metal strips, steel cables, even high tech bolts that had to be cut off with powerful bolt cutters. Coffee and electronics were "high value" loads, always secure and always sealed. Railroads sealed trailer doors with massive 7/16" railroad bolts that get cut off when leaving the rail yard.

With all the rough treatment a trailer gets, it's not uncommon for it to leak. When Schneider had to pay a water damage claim on one of our loads, we learned the hard way the importance of a watertight trailer. A tiny hole in the aluminum skin of our van allowed gallons of water to enter, driven in by 65 mph winds funneling off the cab. Merchandise inside the van wasn't protected from the elements by anything but cardboard, so cartons in the front were plenty soggy.

From then on, we carried silicone caulk in a caulking gun to fix small holes. If we could get inside the trailer, we'd check for leaks by closing the doors to make it dark enough to see pin pricks of sunlight. At night, that's not possible, so you just hope the previous driver inspected it well before he dropped it. And if your trailer is loaded floor to ceiling, the best you can do is look for suspicious holes or parted seams from the outside and seal them.

For trailer housekeeping, we hung a good, wide, stiff, push broom on the back of the cab to sweep out shredded scrap paper, nails, dirt, soap powder, garlic powder, even snow. But once, we had to clean out a trailer that hauled a load of mud-covered used tires. We had no choice but to go to a truck wash where they shoveled and pressure washed the whole inside at Schneider's expense.

Sometimes before sweeping, we had to pull nails out of the oak flooring, like the time we delivered a load of window glass to a car factory in Canada. All the special pallets had been blocked in place by pieces of 2x6 lumber nail-gunned to the floor. After the factory guys removed the pallets, there were still dozens of boards nailed to the floor. Without saying a word, one of the union factory guys handed David a four-foot crowbar and pulled up a folding chair to watch.

Another way to keep a load from shifting is with adjustable nylon webbing load straps. A trailer load stuffed floor-to-ceiling and wall-to-wall with cartons doesn't shift. But a partially-loaded trailer needs to have something to keep the pile from tumbling down during the bumpy ride. Load straps work most of the time. Trailers have rows of holes like adjustable book shelves along the inside where straps hook at appropriate places depending on where the last barrel or paper roll or stack of cartons ends. If the shipper doesn't do it, or doesn't do it right, the driver has to climb in and do it for them. We once took a sealed load of children's books from Madison to Chicago. When we removed the seal and opened the doors for the first time, it was nothing but a jumbled mess of broken boxes and loose books. We had to unload and restack the mess in Chicago for no miles, no pay. It was somewhat ironical that these books were published by Pleasant Company/American Girls, which had been my life in another, previous fast-lane experience.

14

T he steepest part of our learning curve lasted a year. We fine-tuned operational procedures like sliding tandems, but from the beginning, our concept of a job was more than just operations. We had to make the job fun, and creative trip planning was our best tool.

Our motto was to follow the dotted green line. Dotted green lines in the atlas mark "scenic roads." We always opted for the road less traveled, for the skinny road, for the alternate route. Unlike many trucking companies that tell drivers exactly how to get where they're going, Schneider didn't insist on us using designated routes. We were free to get there however we legally could. Of course, they didn't want us spending their gas money on lots of superfluous miles, so there was a company rule which allowed only 10% of miles to be "out of route." We never exceeded that. Sometimes our routes were actually shorter than the all-interstate route. To us it didn't matter how much extra time it took as long as we were on time.

Many drivers, however, make it a strict policy to avoid skinny roads. In bad weather we did, too, because interstates were better plowed and serviced. But on beautiful sunny days, you would see our orange truck on the back roads, going through small towns or scenic wonderlands, often paralleling the interstate by a few miles.

Plenty of legal truck routes which are also dotted green lines run though scenic parks. Hauling firewood from Belgrade, Montana, to Pocatello, Idaho, we drove through a corner of Yellowstone in winter when the elk herds grazed along the highway. High on our list were other scenic roads through Canyon Lands, the Black Hills, Window Rock, Ship Rock, Salt River Canyon, and the Mohave Desert.

To plan our unconventional trips, we kept an accordion folder full of state maps and attractions filed alphabetically. State maps, free at Welcome Centers, have lots more detail than a big road atlas. We'd slip local attraction brochures in along with the state maps. The Hearst Castle literature made it easy enough to call ahead to find out if we could park a tractor there, and using the truck stop guide, we found a nearby truck stop where we could drop our trailer for a half a day.

In Des Moines, where Schneider has an OC, we left the tractor for eight hours of preventive maintenance (PM). With time on our hands, we checked the telephone book to see if a museum or historical building was close by, borrowed the company car for two hours and drove to the city's very nice art museum. It was just enough time to see the Grant Wood exhibit and get back to pick up the truck and continue on our way.

We did a similar thing near Los Angeles on a routine PM. We borrowed the company car to shop for groceries in a Mexican neighborhood grocery store. We liked that store so much that every time we were in Montebello, we shopped there and one Christmas bought big piñatas for our Wisconsin relatives.

Another handy thing about the truck was all the room it had inside the cab to carry big things home, like piñatas. North of Tucson we pulled off onto the shoulder of a state highway on the outskirts and bought one of those big Mexican pottery fireplaces. Strapped it into the upper bunk for the rest of the trip.

In San Diego, after dropping a Sony load, we had four hours before our next assignment, so after a quick call to Sea World to check out the parking situation, we were through the gates and watching killer whales. We even had enough time to walk across the street and do a little bird-watching, a hobby of ours.

Getting to the Sundance Film Festival took a little more planning. Once again, we had time before our delivery deadline to make this stop. We knew the dates of the festival because we regularly read local papers which we'd pick up at truck stops on our trips. Headlined in this one was the film festival's phone number to call for information. We called, told them about our oversized vehicle, asked whether walk-ups like us could buy tickets, and when everything seemed like it would work, we found a small truck stop nearby willing to let us drop a trailer for a few hours. It's true we were oddly conspicuous in a big orange truck parked at the Chamber of Commerce lot in the middle of this posh ski resort town. We didn't care, and it was a great adventure.

When we yearned for a movie in a real theater with delicious stale popcorn, we'd buy a local paper at the truck stop, check times and locations (many multiplex theaters are in malls along major highways) and plan our trip. The best time for a movie was after dropping a trailer, and we were just bobtailing. So if we were in Ontario, California, for instance, we knew there were fifty theaters at the Ontario Mills Mall within twenty minutes of the truck stop, and one of the fifty would fit our schedule. A conventional tractor takes four parking slots in a mall, so even a bobtail wouldn't fit in a really crowded mall. But if you are willing to hike a few blocks, you can generally find parking. And since malls are supplied by big trucks, there is a way in and a way out.

We found that Schneider, if given plenty of notice, made it easy for us to take our time-at-home somewhere else rather than at home. After dropping a load in Los Angeles, we were interested in spending a couple of days renting a car and exploring the San Angeles Mountains and Huntington Museum in Pasadena. So at the end of our two week trip, rather than go back to Wisconsin, we stayed in a Los Angeles motel and called Enterprise Rent-a-Car. The nice thing about Enterprise is that they come to your motel or drop-lot, pick you up, and take you to their office to do the paperwork. On return, they take you back to the motel.

If there's enough time on the load and you work things right, everything comes together in one fantastic trip, like this one:

Subject: Prize winner

Back in January, David came up with such a good idea to improve driver efficiency in a company-wide contest that Schneider presented him with a prize: one night at any Sheraton Hotel at any of their locations and breakfast for two the next morning. We chose Universal City, California, nestled in the hills of Hollywood and adjacent to Universal Studios, a place we sort of wanted to see, and a prize worth $201.

Our adventure west to California started from Escanaba, Michigan, with a load of Mead printing paper on fifteen giant rolls destined for RR Donnelley in Torrance, California. David routed us off the interstate through Dodgeville, Wisconsin, and we stayed on "skinny roads" until Ft. Morgan, Colorado. We saw the insides of many rural towns, their grain elevators, their Cenexes, their bars, their churches, their bank on the corner, their kids on skateboards.

It's hard to stay on skinny roads through the Rockies, but the interstate's thrilling enough when you've got Clear Creek on one side of the divide and the Colorado River on the other -- both at flood stage -- and alpine wildflowers matting every square inch of road cut.

We stayed on the interstate until Utah, one of our favorite western states where we re-discovered US-50, an east-west passage called "The Loneliest Road in America." At dusk, in the Confusion Range, we pulled over on a wide, rocky turnout, ate a can of tamales, hiked up a cobble hillside and looked for fossils.

From there we took a brand new skinny road, green-dotted "scenic" in our atlas that bisects the valley between the Wilson Creek Range and the Egad Range. This is US-93 and is also very lonely. The peaks in the ranges on either side of us were 13,000' but we found a place to park and sleep on the shoulder beside a tiny ranch sixty miles north of Piece. We set the alarm for 04:30 but since it was still dark, slept for another hour.

Our trip next morning led us into Las Vegas. We've driven through Las Vegas dozens of times but never had enough nerve to stop right downtown to visit The Strip. We learned that the best place to stop was Exit #37 at the King 8 Truck Stop. So we fueled up, showered at the regular Schneider stop at Exit #46, drove south to the King 8, parked beside the other trucks, crossed the bridge over I-15 to the New York, New York hotel and casino. Walked around. Lost 50 cents in the slots.

Crossed the street to the Excalibur for a medieval buffet. Lost $1.75. Walked across the skywalk to the Luxor pyramid. Won $4.75. Went to the OmniMax, huge screen showing of "Mir, the Space Station." We left Las Vegas late afternoon and headed for California to cash in our prize. R.R. Donnelly was happy to get their rolls of paper and we were happy to arrange for a rental car and head up through the city of angels and criminals to Universal City.

On the way, we stopped at the La Brea Tar Pits. It was easy to find free parking on the street for a vehicle just a little longer than your legs, so we spent an illuminating two hours checking out the skeletons of the animals unlucky enough to get stuck in asphalt oozing out of the ground.

Then we walked to the Los Angeles Museum of Art, enjoyed the collection of carved miniatures in the Japanese wing, but mostly just admired the architecture and pressed on toward our main objective--the Sheraton Hotel and Universal Studios where we spent the afternoon until closing at 20:00.

We rode the tour rides, ate the food, drank the margaritas, and as evening approached, strolled the shops, minstrels, cafes, theaters. Closing time came and went, the crowd thinned. Alone at last we walked back to the Sheraton at dusk. Nice room, nice breakfast. Nice time.

Call us easily entertained, but pick-up or delivery locations could be intrinsically memorable. One of the best was a central California incinerator. We had a load of old tires, and the destination was purposely unmarked, up into the rounded hills and canyons off I-5 on a skinny private road with wide-eyed cattle wandering across it. After many twists and turns we came to an industrial site, invisible from the highway, surrounded by high slopes. A big sign warned "No cameras" so David surreptitiously pulled ours out and snapped photos in this surreal canyon. Loaders hauled trailers up to the hilltops and dumped the tires onto jumbled mountains of worn out tires. At the bottom of the mountain, a loading station pulled them from the pile and dropped them onto a belt that hauled them up again to the top of a shredder building. Chopped up rubber spewed out the shredder to be carried to the top of another building where it burned — smokeless and secretly in the California hills.

Another time, after dropping our load of empty bottles, we took the Red Hook Brewery plant tour in Woodville, WA. We had a hard time resisting a tiny taste of brew in our complimentary Red Hook tumblers. In central Florida, we faithfully followed directions we knew must be wrong as they led us down a mile long, two-track dirt road to a dusty dead-end parking lot where we picked up a trailer full of pine needles. There wasn't a soul there, just a wrinkled bill of lading stuck in the trailer's nose box to let us know we were in the right place.

In East St. Louis next to a Schneider drop lot, we hung around the old stock yards. Like the rest of East St. Louis, it's in decline; space is cheap. After dropping our trailer we lunched in the renovated stock yard dining hall. A cattle auction was in progress nearby so we dropped in and looked like tourists in the midst of a hundred Illinois and

Missouri ranchers. Making the most of a scheduled delivery or pickup was an easy way to add variety. The only thing predictable about this job was change.

Like other jobs, there was work to be done and the instances we're describing were punctuation points in the process. They made the job fun. No other jobs we'd ever had offered more opportunity to see and learn than this one. Even on the job at the customer's warehouse or factory, the opportunities to learn something new were unlimited. What an education watching trains unload inside cavernous paper plants (Schneider hauls a lot of paper), marveling at high-speed machinery whirling hundreds of aluminum cans per minute, learning how grocery distributors handle thousands of items, smelling vats of tomato sauce cooking in central California.

We found the best way to get inside these factories was to use the plant restroom which is often found by following painted footprints that wind around machinery and across fork lift trails. It was like being on a fifth grade classroom field trip, seeing how paper is made, or how glass windshields are packed.

But make no mistake: there were places people like us wouldn't normally drive into on their own, unescorted in a private vehicle – scary and intimidating industrial sections of Philadelphia, Chicago, East St. Louis, Newark and Los Angeles. But this was, in its own important way, educational and worthwhile. We came away from this job with a new appreciation of how diverse, how complicated, and ethnically mixed our industrial work force is. Again, we can think of no other job that would have given us as much insight into behind-the-scenes America from coast to coast.

On one trip, we'd timed our delivery to arrive after rush hour in downtown Everett, WA, at the Scott paper mill on the shores of Possession Sound. Many logs find their way to this area for processing into lumber and are stacked mountain-high all along the sound. Pulp trucks race in and out with chips to feed the voracious demand for toilet paper and kitchen towels. Paper making machinery is gigantic, as any kid on a field trip knows, and like kids, we watched transfixed.

We were finished by 20:30 and still had no return trip assigned so asked permission to park in a corner of the Scott property to bed down and catch up on sleep. The mill is in a suspicious neighborhood on the docks surrounded by other aging industrial buildings, reconstruction going on here and there, night shift people taking shortcuts through broken chain link fences, strange sounds. We felt it was a good place to sleep as long as the truck doors were locked.

Shortly after 21:00, while still half awake, the cab was rocked back and forth vigorously enough to bring us both to our elbows wondering who was annoying us and what we'd done to deserve it. We'd been awakened several times in the past by lot lizards or by truckers selling hot cameras. Once we had to move because we were blocking access to the truck stop's underground fuel storage and the tanker was there at 03:00 with a fresh supply. But those times they always banged on the cab door to wake us up.

This time David peeled back the curtains and studied the mirrors but could see nobody near the truck. So I urged him to roll down the window, stick his head out to see who'd been pushing us and tell them to get lost. Soon shouts of "earthquake" in the loading dock area confirmed what had happened. We'd blundered to within five miles of the epicenter of a Richter 5.3 quake, Seattle's biggest in fifteen years.

To keep us supplied with similar excitement, I could count on David to live on the edge, like this time:

> Subject: "The Big One"
> William F. Buckley Jr. wrote some books about his yachting experiences. One was about crossing the Atlantic from Boston to the Azores. He was an experienced sailor but this was by far the most ambitious trip he'd attempted in terms of time away

from port, supplies needed, risk of storms, chance for high adventure. The planning process took a year. Throughout he and his crew referred to the trip as "The Big One" and had stationary printed with that as the letterhead.

I was reminded of that earlier this week when our trip plan presented an opportunity to swing wide on the way from Oregon to San Francisco (known as "Shaky" in my profession) and cross the "Big One" of highway bridges, the Golden Gate. There have, of course, been other bridges and tunnels -- George Washington Bridge, the Chesapeake Bay causeway and tunnel, Mackinaw Bridge, Gulfport Beach. But if I had to choose the setting for my only souvenir photo of the orange pumpkin truck, I think I'd choose Golden Gate Bridge with the Pacific in the background, waves crashing on the rocks below, maybe QE2 a mile out.

Like Buckley's crossing, our Big One presented a degree of risk. US-101 in Marin County is not a designated truck route and furthermore it's not on a direct line from our starting point in Portland, ME. If we broke down out there, we'd have some explaining to do as to how we got forty miles out-of-route instead of staying with all the trucks on I-80 across the Bay Bridge. Also, US-101 is not a freeway where it threads its way through the old part of San Francisco so there would be some city driving to do with stoplights, sharp turns, morning rush hour traffic, and many opportunities to get into embarrassing trouble. But The Big One beckoned and I was totally seduced.

As it turned out, timing was everything. I figured that sunrise would be about 06:00 at that latitude, just when rush hour gets going. If we could cross about 05:30, we might sneak through the worst part of the city before 06:00 and still see The Big One, the Pacific, the headlands, the rip tides of the Gate, shipping in the bay, The Presidio. We stopped for the night about one hundred miles north and set the alarm for 03:00. Stopped again fifty miles north to kill off an extra twenty minutes. Took the bold turnoff at Vallejo on Marine World Parkway and CA-37 around the north end of the bay, a two lane highway through extensive marshlands of the San Pablo Bay National Wildlife Refuge. But it was still pitch dark.

At that point, all other trucks vanished. We rejoined the stream of trucks again for a few miles after we turned south on US-101 between Novato and San Rafael in Marin County, but again, south of the I-580 cut-off at San Quentin we were absolutely the only big truck for the next fifteen miles until we crossed Market Street and picked up the freeway system on the other side of central San Francisco. This puzzled me as I had discussed the route with a local driver on the CB radio and he'd led me to believe it was a legal route, just sort of slow. To this day, I wonder if there is a legal restriction, and maybe I'll find out for sure before going there again.

Like so many other times, once committed, to turn back is unthinkable. We blundered on, crossed The Big One and dove into the city on Lombard Street. There was good news/bad news about the timing. I was wrong about sunrise; the bridge was in total darkness, and all we could see was the bridge itself. I was right about rush hour. An hour later would have been disaster. Lombard Street is just a four lane, undivided city street with many stop lights. The right turn onto Van Ness is very sharp and crowded requiring a buttonhook across both lanes. Van Ness goes through the heart of the Civic Center. But at 06:00 no problem. I suppose they see a few long haul semis down there.

Would I do it again? Only if it was surely legal, surely not in rush hour, surely not too far out of the shortest Schneider route, and not in the dark. As it was, even in darkness The Big One had more to offer than a day in the office.

Despite our preference for skinny roads, we did our share of interstate highway travel and, don't let anyone tell you otherwise, some of those highways go through the most scenic country anywhere. We juggled our rest schedule in order to pass awesome scenery during the light of day instead of the middle of the night. Truly, there's nothing much better than I 70 through Colorado's Glenwood Canyon at dawn.

15

It goes without saying: driving is dangerous. Both David and I had perfect driving records as non-commercial drivers. We'd avoided accidents for over thirty years in passenger cars, and danger never was a factor in our decision to be truck drivers. But we underestimated that as a truck driver, you risk it all, all the time. As a team, you spend twenty-four hours a day in what amounts to a crapshoot. You are not in control of every dice roll. Each second behind the wheel is a second when somebody's wheels – yours or theirs -- could wander across the centerline, against a small car, or off the pavement and cause a wreck. That's pretty demanding for only an hour, but all day, every day, it's hard to think of any other profession where exposure to danger is so constant. The ultimate survival skill is to stay alive, healthy and employable.

Some of our inner city and desolate suburban deliveries seemed risky on the face of it. Far more dangerous was driving on the American highway system. For example:

Subject: Body Bag

Almost made it through June without seeing another body bag but it happened

again today between Atlanta and Augusta. Straight, level interstate, light mid-day

Sunday traffic in perfect weather. Trooper flagging traffic to the left lane. Half a dozen rescue workers standing around or moving slow on the right shoulder. Two squad cars and an ambulance. White bundle on a stretcher being slowly loaded into the ambulance. Small blue vehicle buried in the trees way off to the right side. You can tell when everyone's moving slowly that it's too late to do any good.

During our second week of driver training school many of us used the Schneider OC parking lot in Green Bay for parking practice. In the back of that lot were a few wrecked trucks from which maintenance was salvaging parts. Students would stand in front of mangled cabs and speculate about what happened to cause all that chaos. It was not unlike David's Air Force days when pilots studied accident case histories, viewed movies of crash landings, then went out and flew the same kinds of planes.

Throughout our driving years, Schneider bulletin boards featured consciousness-raising reports and photos of accidents. One of the most unforgettable showed a truck that skidded on a twisting, western mountain road, jumped a low stone wall and ended up in a shallow river. The cab was stuffed down into the river, the 53' trailer was still attached, but sticking straight up, its trailer wheels just barely caught on the stone wall. The driver walked away from that one after a little swim.

Driver training lecture sessions included a local deputy sheriff relating his experience as a first responder to an accident where a car had driven under a trailer as the truck driver was attempting to back across a highway into his own driveway for the weekend. Another war story was about the two-man team who left home after a hard weekend partying and only made it 50 miles before the first driver ran into a bridge with his partner already sound asleep in the bunk. They had been "off duty" many hours before driving, so were legal, but not safe. Both died.

Of course, measuring danger is a matter of probabilities. With millions of vehicles on the road every day, only a small percentage gets into trouble. Using careful, defensive, low risk driving practices, a driver can reduce those percentages close to zero. Many drivers have millions of accident free driving miles to their credit. They remind themselves it could happen at any time, they are not immune to the risk, so they stay alert and careful at all times. We tried to stay constantly aware that a moment of inattention at highway speeds could be disastrous. Usually just three feet left or right of center could spell the difference between sleepy boredom and deadly disaster. Not many jobs in America have such a slim safety margin.

As for our actual safety record, I'd already rolled over the OC guard rail, hit one deer out of a herd of seven that came leaping up out of the ditch and ran along side the truck until six decided to jump back in the ditch. One didn't. That accident was considered unavoidable. David chalked up four accidents, two of which cost him monthly bonus checks. If Schneider determined an accident was avoidable, you lose your bonus. He got stuck in the mud, hooked a fuel hose and caused a big expensive fuel spill at a Montana fuel stop, bent a fender on a concrete fuel island, and really crushed the front of an empty trailer while maneuvering near a low truck dock canopy.

Falling asleep at the wheel is almost programmed into the job. Many things about the truck driving industry conspire to keep drivers driving when they ought to be sleeping. Inflexible delivery deadlines, being paid by the mile, lax enforcement of the 10-hour rule, six hour stints unloading cartons at grocery warehouses (sometimes logged as sleep time), and the machismo "I can do anything I want" attitude touted on the CB radio all contribute to a dangerous situation.

A team driver's work schedule is a serious disruption of a person's natural sleep rhythm. It's asking for trouble to put yourself behind the wheel at 3:00 AM when, for most of your life, you are used to being sound asleep at that time. We concentrated on not letting our ambitions jeopardize our safety, or letting drowsiness be ignored. We tried to recognize our own individual symptoms of drowsiness and jump off at the next exit. But it was hard and didn't always work as reliably as it should. There were plenty of times we came close to falling asleep, even with sharp admonitions to each other.

The beginnings of falling asleep are like the beginnings of intoxication. It feels pretty comfortable and pretty good. Soon judgment is impaired, and you begin to think it would feel better to let your head fall back on the backrest instead of periodically bobbing off your chest. You don't think it's a big enough problem to pull over, crawl into the back, and make your partner get out of bed to drive. To counter that natural inclination, we drummed into each other the importance of breaking though the haze and taking action.

Of course, the only sensible action is to stop the truck and sleep. No trick can safely forestall the need for sleep. Caffeine pills might help some drivers for a little while, but eventually caffeine wears off or fatigue becomes undeniable and sleep comes crashing down. We certainly saw plenty of evidence of that. Not only did we follow trucks whose drivers were beginning to drift across centerlines and shoulder lines, there was a memorable sight of a big truck lying on its side on the shoulder of Nebraska I-80 in perfect, dry weather. There is no wider, smoother, straighter, flatter, longer road on earth. The driver obviously dozed off, drifted to the right shoulder, woke with a start when he heard the steers hit gravel or mile posts slapping the grille, and yanked the steering wheel back to the left, dumping the top heavy rig on its right side. With examples like that every week, we eagerly got out of bed and drove whenever necessary to relieve a sleepy partner.

We found the best solution to manage drowsiness was to manage the schedule. We developed a work/sleep schedule to help prevent drowsiness. For us, that meant no more than a four hour shift behind the wheel, frequent naps for the off-duty driver, and three or four hours of quality sleep after midnight everyday. We'd find some place to pull off, even an on-ramp shoulder, which was absolutely against Schneider rules, to rest.

If we happened to be near a rest area or truck stop, we'd park upwind of all the other trucks to avoid inhaling diesel exhaust.

In the logbooks, we used the "split break" rule that allows the eight-hour sleep break to be made up of two periods in the sleeper. We felt that we were safest that way. We know teams who split the day into a daylight shift and a night shift. During time at home, the night shift person makes it a point to read books all night and sleep a lot during the day to keep her clock from being re-set.

Even with a liberal amount of rest time between shifts in the driver's seat, the mind wants to go blank and start to shutdown. It was important for us to have a good radio and interesting music and plenty of books-on-tape. It had been our ambitious self-improvement plan to catch up on a misspent lifetime without books. It didn't take long to find out that reading a paragraph in a bouncing truck was possible, but no way could we read an entire page, let alone an entire book, without getting carsick. We solved the problem by using our local library to reserve two week's worth of books-on-tape, and we had enough entertainment and education in our three years of driving to make up for many years of laziness.

Although it was strictly against Schneider rules to wear earphones in the truck, what I did to make the listening experience better was to buy earphones with electronic feedback noise suppression. The theory was that if you wore earphones, you couldn't hear sirens. Turns out that simply isn't true; actually, you can hear sirens better because only the white background noise of the engine is silenced. So, to listen to music or audio books through those wonderful earphones was welcome relief even though it wasn't enough to drown out David yelling from the bunk when I missed gears.

During our driving career, we listened to eighty books-on-tape. Some were ten or eleven hours long and books we'd never have attempted under normal circumstances. One of us would get a head start listening to a book on his/her shift and the other followed a few cassettes later. That way we listened to the same book about the same time so we could talk about it as we listened. It's a rare opportunity to read on the job, but driving is one job where it's encouraged. If our books were overdue and there were fines to pay, we paid them willingly. It was cheap enough entertainment and education. And it probably kept us from falling asleep.

If the thought of falling asleep at the wheel doesn't remind you this is a dangerous job, then slippery roads will. Summer and winter driving are like night and day, especially where your route goes through elevations -- near the Rockies, Appalachians, Sierras, or Smokies. October through April, we spent a lot of time planning a route to avoid the worst of it, sometimes successfully. Other times, we had no choice but to bail out and park the truck:

Subject: Winter Driving

Our vow is to get off the road whenever conditions deteriorate. We carry enough food for several days. No sense pushing it, just get off before the exit ramps become impassable, and wait for the sun to shine. Thus armed with food and a strategy, we boldly turned toward Billings, Montana, October 18th with 44,000 pounds of Girl Scout cookies from New Jersey. High country temperatures were down to 10 degrees F, with mountain snow. Would this be our first test?

It didn't take long to find out. Around Scott's Bluff, Nebraska, the land starts to rise as flat wheat and sugar beet fields give way to buttes, mesas and canyons, and some of the scattered clouds seemed to be sweeping the ground. Our fancy electronic digital inside/outside thermometer read 40 degrees F, but within two hours we were in and out of blinding flurries. Snow was accumulating on the grassy ground, but the roadway was so warm, it stayed clear, either wet or dry but no problem.

By the time you reach Casper, Wyoming, I-90 gets into some pretty high elevations. The highway was snow-covered and icy in patches, interspersed with bare pavement. Shelley drove until 22:00 while I slept, then we both slept for two more hours before I started out again about midnight.

More snow. Here and there trucks were parked at on-ramps. I was surprised at how much snow was sticking to the pavement but the highway department had been spreading red sand on the road, and there was still plenty of traffic, so I kept going, looking for the final clue that would send us creeping off the road to wait it out. These were the exact conditions we'd sworn not to keep driving in, but the last nap had used all but two hours of available time to reach our destination in time for a 07:00 appointment. Should I use those two hours now and give the road crews more time to sand, or keep trying to get through before too much snow accumulated and shut down the interstate? If the road was open and other trucks kept driving, how could we explain that we'd stopped and missed a Schneider appointment?

In the Air Force we called it "get-home-itis." It's a mental disorder that forces a pilot to take off in bad weather or keep flying into bad weather because he's on his way home and can't wait. Same problem in trucking, but this trip we were not going home, just making good on a company commitment and trying not to waste our time by earning $0.30/mile at zero miles per hour.

This time the final decision was taken out of my hands. Big sign with flashing yellow lights: I-90 closed 1.5 miles ahead. All traffic use Exit #90. I got off and found just three trucks and a motor home ahead of me, looking for a place to park. The "road closed" sign had just been turned on.

We sent a satellite message to Schneider to postpone our delivery appointment indefinitely and to phone the Montana Highway Department to get an idea when the road would re-open. Got our answer: 65 vehicle pileup ahead, not known how long before re-opening. We went to bed at 02:00 with no alarm set, CB off.

Woke up at 06:00 to find most of the other trucks gone. Road had been re-opened at 05:00, but we'd enjoyed four hours of guilt-free sleep. Back out on the interstate, conditions were rotten. Snow had stopped, but there was very little sand, and it was fifty miles of packed snow and ice before the road dried up at lower altitudes. Once again, we'd kept rolling on treacherous roads. A family conference is called for. Keeping fingers crossed just ain't going to do it in the long run.

Despite skid pad training, sometimes there isn't much a driver can do to regain control on an icy road once a skid starts. There's no way to practice skidding with all the variables you encounter in a real situation — like wind, load size, road grade, obstacles, speed, and driver agility. Training helped to avoid the start of a skid, but a semi-trailer rig slaloms in more than one direction, has a lot of inertia and needs a lot of traction. A very light load will not give the tractor drive tires much traction. That makes it easier to get stuck on an uphill grade, or start a drive wheel skid. After you factor in what's between you and the end of the skid, the only completely safe way to go on ice is not to go.

The first wreck skidding out-of-control toward you is one you never forget. This email of David's says it all:

Subject: Wreck

Experienced our first major winter driving incident this noon. The good news is that Shelley and I are okay. But you should've seen the two other guys. Wrecked their trucks and blocked I-80 for half a day.

The scene is Sherman Mountain just west of Cheyenne, Wyoming. It's the highest point of elevation on I-80 between the George Washington Bridge and the Oakland Bay Bridge -- 8,640 feet. Weather was cloudy, and I was having my midday nap. Shelley was driving east from Seattle. We had changed our route westbound and again eastbound this week because of snow packed roads in Washington and Montana. Feeling pretty smug to get out and back without being stuck. Only one more pass to cross and all of the high altitude road would be behind us.

A plaintive "Daaaaviiid" from the driver's seat roused me from my slumber. Squinting into the bright overcast I saw we were in a solid line of semis slowly but steadily grinding down to zero miles per hour on the steepest part of the Sherman climb — two lanes in each direction with almost no shoulder. A 3' high concrete barrier separates eastbound from westbound. Everyone was in the main left-hand lane straddling tracks of wet ice. The right lane was white hard-packed snow.

Trucks ahead of us were losing traction and bringing the whole line to a halt. Some hot shots with heavy loads had gone around in the right lane but already some of those were spinning out too. Shelley flipped the power divider switch that locks drive axles together, downshifted at five mph, but couldn't keep the drive wheels from spinning. With her last bit of momentum, she crept over to the right hand lane and set the parking brakes.

Everyone else came to a dead stop in the left lane and waited for the trucks up hill to get sorted out. But Shelley and I got out the chains and hung one on each side. There was lively debate on the CB about "hanging iron." Some drivers refuse to do it, seeing it as a threat to their masculinity. Shelley and I needed the practice and we were safely out of the way in the right lane. Nobody was going anywhere at the time anyway. We tried and failed to get moving with the two chains, so hung two more.

After twenty minutes, traffic was crawling along single file. It was my turn to drive, and with four chains on, had no trouble. Here and there drivers were spinning out and hanging chains but most made it on bare rubber if they stayed in the groove where the ice was intermittent. Our chains kept coming unbuckled so I got over in the right lane and put duct tape on the buckles. For a long time there was no traffic coming the other direction so something had stopped that side, too.

Sherman Pass has a double top like a camel with two humps, a gentle half-mile dip between them. We topped the first hump and the problem changed to going downhill without jack-knifing. A couple of guys went by at forty mph, but most of us were happy at twelve. We'd been watching the downhill traffic on the other side and they were creeping, too. But here in the saddle between humps a couple of trucks going westbound opposite us got seduced. After finally getting through the westbound traffic jam, they got up a good head of steam rolling down their first hump to carry them right up the second hump.

Like they say, "It all happened so quickly." A westbound truck lost traction on its drive wheels coming up the hump and his trailer wagged across both lanes just ahead of us on the other side of the concrete barrier. At the same time, a complete idiot in a newish Kenworth conventional tractor was barreling past him. The idiot smashed into the back of the first trailer and came careening down the center barrier, his driver's side fender stripping off a hundred feet of reflector posts mounted every two feet on the barrier top. I remember being surprised by the violence of the impact. Truck pieces somersaulted in the air in slow motion disintegration.

He was sliding along the concrete median barriers straight for us. I checked around for non-existent escape routes. But he stayed on his side of the barrier and came to a stop just a truck length ahead of us. The CB lit up. I joined in to suggest the two trucks ahead of me should move past the wreck a little distance before stopping to lend assistance. They did, and I kept creeping toward a stopping point that would be easy to get out of when the crisis passed. The first cab wasn't damaged much and the driver was on the CB, but the Kenworth was a wreck. We couldn't see the driver behind all the crumpled steel. But as I crept past he stumbled out of his steaming wreck and over the barrier rubbing his elbow and taking a look at what was left of his truck. Cowboy boots, flannel shirt, Willie Nelson hair, many years of professional driving experience no doubt. I yelled at him, "You got a partner in there?" He lamely wagged his head no, and we got out of there.

But we'd learned another winter driving safety tip: if you're in a passenger car around a lot of big semis that seem to be bunching up, stay clear. Some fools in passenger cars with four-wheel drive were weaving in and out of all this mess while the whole event was happening. For them, it could have been curtains.

Again, good driving procedure and decision-making can minimize these risks. On wet blacktop roads, other semis might speed by us as we drove more slowly and increased our following distance. If it meant that our following distance gap kept being filled by a reckless driver, we'd just fall back and widen the gap again. We'd seen too many hydro-foiling cars and trucks to discount wet roads as less dangerous than icy ones.

Being caught up in natural disasters happens more often when you cross the country as many times as we did. Ice storms, earthquakes, floods, fires and landslides may be local newspaper articles to the rest of the country but were headline events for us.

Subject: Donner Pass

Between Sacramento and Stockton in the flat farmland of the Central Valley, all northbound traffic disappeared. The fields east of the highway began to look more and more flooded, and soon water was covering the northbound slow lane. We crossed a branch of the San Joaquin River and saw the hole in the dike that caused the problem. They channel these rivers through aqueducts fifteen feet above the surrounding countryside. Good idea.

Ten miles later we passed several miles of backed up northbound traffic being diverted to Hwy 99 which is a good freeway paralleling I-5. The northbound lane of I-5 had been acting as a dike to protect the southbound lanes. For the next twenty miles southbound trucks warned northbound trucks to get off in Stockton and take 99 to avoid the backup. We made mental notes to use 99 the next day when we returned with our new load from Los Angeles to Akron.

But further south we heard radio reports of a new flood developing near Fresno and Madera. Soon the CB was full of stories from truckers who had been diverted off Hwy 99. So the next day we went north as far as Stockton on I-5, then crossed to 99 two exits before the mandatory detour and avoided all trouble. The CB definitely saved us some hours that trip.

We were headed toward the Sierra Nevadas where the Donner emigrant party got famous by getting stranded up there in "freak" winter weather and to survive, they ate each other. The Donner Pass and Emigrant Gap are more recently famous for being closed by frequent snowstorms, inconveniencing the weekend gamblers and skiers from Sacramento and Frisco. Thus, our focus turned from flood problems to snow problems. The only route other than I-80 to the Tahoe area, US 50, washed out New Years Day and will be out for weeks.

Official radio announcements reported snowfall at the summit. Use of chains was still optional. Sure enough, about midnight a mile from the summit, snow filled the air and a half-inch covered the bare pavement. Trucks were still getting though "barefoot" so we kept going. Next morning chains were mandatory at Donner Pass.

But that bad news was behind us as we headed, pre-dawn, into Reno next day. We crept through the gaudy city on I-80's icy pavement and past a construction crew doing some kind of heavy earth moving in the westbound lanes. Westbound traffic was diverted onto an eastbound lane for a few hundred yards. Twenty miles later we stopped for a break and picked up a newspaper. The headline: "PIT THREATENS I-80". The edge of an old gravel pit had been washed away. It looked like a big bite out of a forty-foot high cliff. The chomp extended to the edge of the interstate shoulder where we'd just rolled by six feet from the abyss.

The State Patrol and DOT 1-800 phone numbers for road condition reports turned out to be hopelessly out of date and useless. The best source of information for trip planning in those days was the Weather Channel on cable television. All winter, Schneider OC's and some truck stops had a television permanently tuned to the weather. Weather Channel forecasts were indispensable and, if possible, we would trip plan to a highway less likely to stop us dead in our tracks.

But, because we're only human, sometimes we made mistakes:

Subject: Stuck

Easter Sunday we started a trip from Phoenix to Akron. The smart winter route is I-40 through Flagstaff, Oklahoma City, St. Louis, etc. But winter was over and this was a rare opportunity to chose a (new for us) route that cuts across the southeast corner of Colorado on US-160 through the San Juan mountains. With only a quarter of a full load, about 10,000 pounds, we would fly up the hills and have no trouble on the down slopes. Numerous checks on the weather channel reported snow just around Salt Lake City. By getting an early start (04:00), we'd have time to fuel and shower, pick up the load in Phoenix and still get to see northern Arizona and southern Colorado as far as the foothills before dark. Then we'd cross eastern Colorado and Kansas on two-lane US-50 under a full moon.

We stopped at Flagstaff's Little America truck stop to check the weather channel one final time. Just to be sure, at the last chance to bail out in Chimney Rock, Colorado, we stopped at an Indian casino and telephoned the official road closings report. Everything was open.

Approaching 10,000' Wolf Creek Pass, the westbound trucks warned us to get our chains on because it was snowing at the top and a U-Haul truck was stuck sideways across the east bound lane and once stopped, we'd need chains to get moving again.

David asked, "Is it open or closed, Westbound?"

"She's open, but the wrecker has some mopping up, so there's a delay. You'll definitely need to hang some jewelry."

This is what we had come to see. US-160 snakes up the face of a 3,000' cliff grooved by a series of remarkable switchbacks. It's a great sight and we timed our arrival for the last hour before sunset, but the freak snow squall was obscuring everything. Moist clouds funneling up the valley from west to east had created a ten mile diameter snow storm, too small for any weather reports to report. Tough luck.

So we parked at the chain-up area about the 6,000' mark, ten miles from the top and put a cable chain on each of the four outside drive tires. Last year we got stuck, along with everyone, on Sherman Pass in Wyoming. Just four chains did a great job of getting us out of that, so we didn't put any on the four inside tires this time either. It only took twenty minutes to put on the outside chains, but the insides are harder to reach, messy, and a nuisance.

Schneider's idea of "chains" is really a web of steel cables that wrap around the tire. They meet the legal requirement to carry chains in the western states, but they don't guarantee you'll go in snow, as we were soon to find out.

Right there is where we made the bad decision. We were in a big, flat, safe parking area. The snow squall was the type that soon blows away. The conditions were getting worse, not better. We could always use more nap time. But several factors were scratching an itch. We were playing hooky from the normal truck route. And darkness would soon obscure the mountain views we had come so far to see.

Starting up the hill, we quickly hit the snow line. About an inch of wet snow and it was still falling. However, there was no hard-packed layer of white ice or packed snow for the chains to bite into. Just slushy, slippery snow and ice. Within two miles we started to spin our wheels and slow down. We got over onto the shoulder before whining to a halt.

We put out our warning triangles, attached the rest of the nuisance chains to the inside drive wheels and gave it a little test to see if we were free. Our situation was a wee precarious. The shoulder was on the wall side of the road, not the drop off side, but there was a little drainage ditch three feet from the right wheels and the shoulder was sloped toward it. Attempts to move forward resulted in the drive wheels slipping and sliding sideways toward the ditch as we inched forward. Couldn't make it. After walking around the stuck truck a few times and up and down the highway to assess the slip/slope line, we very carefully tried backing out into the lane of traffic to try it out there, but each touch on the brakes backing downhill caused the unchained trailer tires to slip sideways toward the ditch. We were not getting out into the traffic lane, just closer to the ditch.

The only way to get out to the track plowed just minutes earlier would be to put it in reverse and boldly idle right back, letting the engine brake keep the speed under control. Once away from the ditch it would be okay to touch the brakes. The tractor had to be inched closer to the ditch as we backed up so the trailer would aim away from the ditch. Worst case: we'd get the tractor stuck in the ditch, but if the only way out of the snow was to be pulled by a wrecker, being in a ditch and a snow bank would be no trouble for the kind of wrecker we'd need. There was almost no traffic coming up or down the hill, so we wouldn't trouble anyone by blocking the uphill lane for the time required to line up and give it one last try. If it didn't work, it would be no trouble backing down onto the shoulder again.

All went according to plan. We picked up our triangles, got lined up in the traffic lane, got moving in first gear, shifted into second gear, traveled one hundred yards in the right direction. But the drive wheels were slipping half the time and the cheap cable "chains" don't like that very much. A left inside chain broke off and there went twelve percent of our traction. We ground to a halt again. If the road surface had been snow packed, if we had been carrying a heavier load, if we'd put all eight chains on, if we'd been there two hours sooner, whatever, no problem.

Now, this was a total screw-up. What would Schneider think of our off-the-wall route? They were bound to find out. They'd have to pay the bill for towing unless it was sort of cheap and then we might pay cash. Could the wrecker handle it? We were on a steep climb, on a tilted shoulder, and snow plows had built up quite a bank of snow around us. How long would it take? Would we be late arriving in Akron? Our biggest worry (besides crashing) has always been the embarrassment of getting stuck in a dead-end street someplace, having to call the police to supervise a U-turn or a long back up. There was only one way out of this one. No way were we going to back down this hill, slipping with each touch of the brakes, around hairpin curves, oncoming traffic, for god knows how many miles to the next wide spot for a U-turn. We were stuck in more ways than one.

Sent word on the CB for the wrecker to come get us out of this mess. Meanwhile, skiers in their 4x4's on the way to Wolf Creek Ski Area sped by effortlessly one after the other. Well after dark the big wrecker arrived, hooked onto our tow hook with a twelve-foot nylon strap, and gently took up the slack. We both applied the power and jumped out of that snow bank like jack rabbits.

At that point in the plowed lane we might have proceeded on our own, but we stayed hooked up all the way to the top. The wrecker driver asked that we keep our headlights off so he could see in his mirrors without being blinded. We coordinated gearshifts so we wouldn't lose momentum and zigzagged seven miles up the mountain at 25 mph twelve feet behind the wrecker. Too much power and we'd overtake, too little and we'd slow down. Any angle on the tow rope might yank the wrecker into a spinout, so steering was critical. Twice the wrecker driver encouraged overtaking semi-trucks with real chains to pass us. Maybe he knew the road so well he could feel oncoming traffic. Surely he couldn't see around all the curves.

At the top we signed the wrecker's bill for Schneider's account, $350 for a half hour's work, and shook his happy hand. We were the third big truck that afternoon, along with four cars and two U-Haul trucks. We'd been stuck four hours.

Two more broken chains, wrapped around the axles, had to be removed at the top. Then we crept down the next two miles at fifteen mph to a chain removal area below the snow line. The sky was clear on that side, the moon was full, all was well. Shelley drove two more hours through the moonlight but David went to bed and slept six hours.

The CB radio, in spite of the bad rap I give it, can be an important source of current information about the road ahead. That's the main reason we kept it turned on, so you can hear this:

In a truck stop, Stewart, Iowa
"Eastbound, how's I-80 going west?"

"Well, she's greasy. You got a big rig in the middle at the 85 [mile marker] with a 4-wheeler under it. You got a wiggle wagon blocking the left lane by the pickle park at 82. About the 20 she's just wet and after Omaha she's clear all the way to Wyoming. You got parking space in that truck stop? I'm gittin' off. No fun, 30 mile an hour. Fuck this shit."

I-80 near Stewart, Iowa

"Hit the brakes! Hit the brakes! Truck across the road. Eastbound hit the brakes! Slidin' down the right lane. God Damn!"

"What's the mile marker for that wreck eastbound?"

"Where's the wreck?"

"Just like a dumb shit driver to give everything but the location."

"Westbound, what's over yer shoulder?"

"Good news eastbound, you might get to the 105. Bad news, everyone's stopped there, can't get up the hill. Worse news, 80's closed by wrecks at Des Moines--maybe you can get around on 235."

"Which truck stop's got the best restaurant between here and the 105?"

A pickup in the median is one of the first clues there's trouble. Like hawks, we'd watch the outdoor digital thermometer mounted on the dash. When it hovered around the freezing point and there was no spray coming off our tires or the vehicle's in front of us, it was time to jump ship. Just about then, we'd see the first lightweight pickup truck in a ditch or flipped in the median.

Sometimes the decision to get off the road wasn't ours to make. Out west the DOT road crew drops a barricade across the interstate to block the on-ramp. But other times it's a tough judgment call.

If falling asleep at the wheel or black ice doesn't get you thinking that maybe truck driving isn't for you, try driving in high crosswinds. On just a ten-mile stretch of I-80 east of Omaha, we passed seventeen tractor-trailers lying like kid's broken toys on their sides or in the ditch. They'd all been blown over by a thunderstorm a few hours earlier. A van is designed for 47,000 pounds. If it has only 8,000 pounds of empty aluminum cans, it's a disaster waiting to happen.

If falling asleep at the wheel and slippery roads and high winds don't convince you that driving is dangerous, a heart attack might. On the road, it's so easy and so much fun to indulge on heart-stopping truck stop food. There is a huge temptation to treat yourself to a big dinner after all day in the truck. Averaging almost a thousand miles a day, pretty soon you've gone more than 200,000 miles per year past billboards dripping with ice cream cones and mouth-watering close-ups of broiled steaks.

Rarely is there an exit without food, especially cookie-cutter franchise food. For all the reasons mentioned above, we stopped at our share, aiming when we could for mom-and-pop cafes with truck parking. After the first four months as new drivers, we saw how quickly our weight was ballooning so we made it a policy to bring food from home instead of eating every meal in cafes or truck stops. At least the portions were more reasonable, nothing was fried, and it was cheaper. We had a portable 12-volt lunch-box type heater that plugged into the cigarette lighter. A little water in the bottom of that would steam heat hot dogs, an unopened can of soup, pork and beans, tamales, vegetables – almost any canned food. It took an hour, but it was hot, tasty enough, and if we had fresh fruit, balanced.

Here's my e-mail about road food:

Subject: Recipes on the road

Prior to a trip, I take myself to Woodman's if I'm in Madison, the Superior Market if I'm in Montebello, California, or Food Lion, Ralph's, Lucky, Winn Dixie, Giant, etc., if we're "away." It used to be that David and I shopped together. Six weeks ago after his large-girth Levis failed to zip shut, I shop alone. He's settled into a simple diet of Slim Fast milk shakes and solid food supplements, like apples.

At Woodman's, I pack a grocery cart with: ready-made salad, lite Frankfurters, four bananas bought singly and in various stages of ripeness, two Braeburn apples, red grapes, a watermelon quarter, broccoli, cherry tomatoes, Snackwell's chocolate yogurts, Health Valley granola bars, Pamela's wheat-free pecan shortbread cookies, fat-free Quaker Oats mini rice cakes, Barbara's fat-free oatmeal raisin mini cookies, popcorn, lite Pringles, coke in plastic bottles, a quart of 2% milk, Rice Krispie treats in the large family-size box (forty-eight individually wrapped), deli potato salad, baked-not-fried tortilla chips, Lunch Buckets of corned beef hash, chili, Dinty Moore beef stew, Bumblebee tuna fish packed in water, UV boxed low-fat milk, After the Fall boxed juices, Nestea, peppermints, Ultra Slim Fast for David -- both bottled and dry. And cottage cheese. Oh, and blueberries.

We've learned how to squirrel away a commissary's worth of provisions inside the truck. It's just that you sleep right on top of the ripening bananas and after three days of steady ripening finally eat all three at once just to get rid of the overwhelming aroma.

Our plug-in Igloo refrigerator does a good job keeping things thirty degrees cooler than the outside temp, but when you want the blueberries and not the tuna fish, and the blueberries are behind the tuna, then it's murder. So if you happen to have fantasized about the blueberries and cottage cheese and only the tuna rolls out when the Igloo door is opened, then be prepared to unpack the whole mess onto the bed around the sleeping David who doesn't have to eat anymore because of Slim Fast.

Hot meals are becoming increasingly popular. Slim Fast does allow one real meal a day, so David shares whatever I'm having. Lunch Bucket chili with a side of mini rice cakes, Coke to drink, and a Snackwell's chocolate yogurt is a nice dinner. Steamed broccoli is one our new hot creations. Our plug-in cooker lined with aluminum foil (stowed in the crack between the mattress and the cab wall) with a teaspoon of water and six flowerets of broccoli cooks in just twelve minutes. When we eat out (about one third of the time) we squeeze into the tiniest cafe parking lots in the most out-of-the-way places we can find, join the regulars and feast on huevos rancheros, BBQ, potato pancakes, or whatever the house specialty is. No wonder my weight, blood pressure and cholesterol are hitting new levels.

Added to this bounty of food, there was no way to exercise. We made some half-assed attempts. We regularly parked the truck some distance from the rest stop door so we could walk briskly, even jog a few steps. But in winter or rain, our zeal to stay fit was overwhelmed by our zeal to stay warm and dry. David bought an EZ Crunch, a simple rubber-band-powered TV special offer for doing crunches (sit-ups in the seated position). He hoped that would give him a rippling six-pack of abdominals, but for that to happen, he'd have do more than hope. Finally, we started doing isometric exercises as we drove. We'd try to keep our abs flexed from one bridge to another along interstates, or if there weren't bridges, from one exit to the next. Nice effort, but no effect.

Schneider has work-out rooms in many of its OC's, and it would have been a smart move to use those. They were convenient, free, and almost always empty. But as a team, it would have cost us $20/hour to be in the gym instead of on the road. Not gonna happen.

16

We lived our dream job in the world of long haul truck driving from February, 1996, until February, 1999, interrupted once by a five month leave of absence to move into a new house. During thirty-one months of driving we were fully a part of that world, and we came away with a good sense about which parts of the job were dreamlike and which were nightmarish. Basically a simple job, truck driving nevertheless is a complicated equation that factors in such things as unorthodox lifestyle, company management skills (or lack of), and government regulations.

Generally, we reflect on those days as an uncommon experience we were glad to have had and content with our choices that enabled us to do it. We gained a valuable education, saved a little money, enjoyed some relaxed and happy days, weeks, months, and came away with indelible memories.

But specifically, we bitched about a lot of things. Shedding white collars for blue ones, we expected some, but not all, of this. Hour to hour and day to day, there were unavoidable obstacles, some miserable working conditions, difficult people and situations. Anyone contemplating a future career in truck driving might find guidance in our experience.

Part of the trouble is that "paid miles" were almost always less than odometer miles. We drove the miles, but we didn't get paid for all of them. Industry uses a mileage guide to determine paid miles but it uses "as the crow flies" miles rather than real distance traveled on legal truck routes. This practice is unfair and is the sort of arbitrary treatment that causes workers to turn to a union for help.

Dependence on mileage pay makes paychecks vary wildly from period to period due to factors totally beyond the driver's control. "Slow freight" is one excuse for letting a driver sit for half a day waiting for the next assignment. Other times assignments are just intrinsically good or bad because of built-in efficiencies or inefficiencies. For instance, some weeks feature a string of long delays for live load assignments which results in low total mileage compared to hot weeks with efficient drop and hooks and, therefore, high total mileage. Drivers have no control over the types of assignments.

Delays, regardless the reason, stop a driver dead in his tracks, unable to earn mileage pay, even though he is in the truck and at the ready. Many drivers complain with their feet, walking out to try a different company with better loads, more miles. We suspect new recruits get special assignments for awhile to help them feel good about their new company. After a month or two the good loads get scarce.

There should be some incentive pay for delays, for sticking with a company until assignments become more profitable. Such a company expense would simultaneously provide an incentive for office workers to keep trucks and drivers moving efficiently. Here's an example of time-wasting:

Subject: Maintenance

Last Wednesday Shelley started the tractor and backed it out of its parking spot to bring it closer for loading. Halfway out of the slot I could see her leaning out the driver side door, beckoning me to come help.

With typical spousal impatience I hollered something basic like, "Push the clutch to the floor," but that was exactly the problem. The clutch was on the floor, and would not spring back up. Broken throw-out bearing. Six to eight hour repair. We could use a loaner [unassigned tractor] for our next delivery and return it the next day.

So, we transferred all our stowed gear from our truck to the loaner, backed the new tractor to the loaded and newly-shoed trailer and hooked it up. It had just received six new tires but I walked around with the hammer just the same thumping each tire, and son-of-a-gun, one of the two old tires was flat. We waited in line to drive through the tire bay, got a seventh new tractor tire, and received a satellite message to contact the fuel desk about shuttling an additional tractor to Green Bay.

Schneider was expanding service to Weyerhaeuser and needed a specialized (flatbed) tractor at their Green Bay yard by 06:00 next morning. It had been on its way up there but the delivery driver inexplicably left it in Milwaukee and disappeared. Everyone was so happy to have discovered a team to run this errand. We would save the day.

We were scheduled to go through Green Bay on our way to the next delivery location, a Kimberly Clark plant, so it was reasonable to expect a team to separate long enough to deliver a tractor one-hundred-eighty miles further up the route. I was eager to show what good sports and productive drivers we were. Shelley could drive the bobtail; I could drive the new loaner tractor with our load. At Green Bay she was to park the bobtail, jump back in our loaner, and we'd be on our way. Simple.

Shelley was apprehensive about being all alone for the first time in a big truck. But with me behind her, and with no trailer attached, she was reluctant but willing. First I had to get inside the door of the Weyerhaeuser tractor because again, the keys were lost. Maintenance manufactured a new key; it opened the door but didn't turn the ignition. They installed a new ignition switch but the electrical system was dead.

Major maintenance required. They towed it to the shop while we ate supper and phoned Green Bay to do a little whining. Another half hour delay and our regular load would be late, arriving after its midnight deadline. Maybe we should leave the Weyerhaeuser tractor for someone else to deliver after it was feeling better and truly fixed. But to Michelle, our boss, it was very important to get this tractor to Weyerhaeuser by 06:00 the next morning, so she would make sure Kimberley Clark allowed us some extra time to deliver our load of bleached recycled paper bales to Marinette, Wisconsin. Dejected, we ordered dessert and watched a Western in the video lounge.

When we went to the garage to check on progress, the cab was jacked up, wires were pointing in all directions around the batteries and voltage regulator, and the mechanic was noncommittal about what the fix would be, or how long it might take. It was now 20:30 on a day when we had planned to depart by 15:00 to make a four hour run. Snow was predicted that night at Marinette, and we saw our plans for an early delivery and good night's sleep beginning to evaporate.

We called Michelle again to do some serious whining. We already had one strange new loaner tractor to deal with. We had not one, but two new locations to find in the dark. We'd been up all day. It was going to snow. With the side trip to Weyerhaeuser our load would already be an hour late and the mechanic didn't know how much more time he would require. That truck might never start tonight.

They talked it over in Green Bay and decided that one of us should run the Kimberly Clark load to Marinette, pickup the new loaded trailer, and meet the other driver next morning at Green Bay. Shelley would wait in Milwaukee as long as it took for the Weyerhaeuser tractor to get fixed, then run it up to Green Bay where I would pick her up on the way back south next day. I said I didn't think that was for us. Shelley said maybe in a million years. Michelle parked us on hold while she made some calls, then came back and let us off the hook. We left the dead Weyerhaeuser tractor behind and headed north through very light lake effect snow showers that didn't bother much at all, and Kimberly Clark let us sleep in their yard after we dropped the trailer at 01:30 next morning.

By 05:30 we were on our way again, this time with 23,000 pounds of toilet paper and a bill of lading stating a next day midnight delivery deadline in New Milford, Connecticut, and "THIS IS HOT--PLEASE RUSH" stamped in red. We had thirty hours to make a twenty-four hour drive. No sweat. We'd requested 09:00 completion time for our tractor's new clutch throw-out bearing job. We'd be getting the loaner back to Milwaukee about 09:30 to move our stuff back into our own truck, couple to the load, and go for a drive through Pennsylvania, New York, and Connecticut.

But Milwaukee maintenance had more surprises for us. Our truck cab was still jacked up, drive shafts, shift linkages, fuel/water separator, oil filter, batteries and wiring were all over the floor. "Maybe she'll be done by 14:00," the mechanic said. It had been in maintenance twenty-four hours and our six to eight hour job still needed another four and a half hours to finish. If all went well we'd hit Chicago about 16:00 just in time for the afternoon rush. This trip that had started on April Fool's day was getting to be a bad joke.

We'd arrived a half hour too late for breakfast, so ate an early lunch, ran some errands, and checked back with maintenance at noon. The mechanic looked up from his euchre hand, pursed his lips, and suggested we check back after 14:30--he'd have a firm schedule by then. Shelley and I discussed the pros and cons of pushing for the loaner for one more trip. I got on the phone again, not yet a professional driver, but I was sure turning into a professional whiner.

17

A JB driver had a trailer come uncoupled but he kept on driving until a Smoky Bear stopped him, took him back to show him the JB trailer upside down in the ditch. "Is that your trailer?" "No officer, my trailer had wheels on the bottom."

That was a Schneider driver making fun of their competition, J. B. Hunt. We'd hear put-downs and jokes on the CB, but if you asked us what the truck driving community was like, we couldn't tell you. We didn't know any other truck drivers. We were in the truck, driving. Solo drivers spend time hanging around truck stops, but team drivers are paid to drive almost constantly. So our sense of community came over the CB. It could be entertaining, even educational. David had a long talk with an egg hauler.

Subject: Eggs

Going east across Ohio on US-30 late one night I was listening to two drivers discussing their egg delivery schedules. After about ten minutes of this I butted in to ask how many eggs they could get on a semi, and if they had to be extra careful to avoid bumps in the road to keep a smooth ride. Here's what I learned.

Ninety-thousand eggs is a good load. Eggs are packed on flats. The flats are stacked up in cases. The cases are stacked up on pallets. They are delivered to processors who grade them for quality and size and then process egg products or repack in retail one-dozen cartons. Drivers have to help load and unload. A good bump in the road can smush the bottom cartons, but more eggs are broken in loading and unloading than in transit. Still, most processing plants keep snapshots on the wall of some of the most memorable sights they see when they open the back doors of a new truckload arrival.

These two drivers recalled some of their biggest messes. A driver opened his back doors before backing to the dock and noticed the top of the load had shifted forward due to some heavy braking. He tried to even it out by bumping the dock sort of hard, and unloaded the back stack of cases right onto the warehouse floor.

Another was unloading a pallet full of cases with a pallet jack that tipped into a hole in the floorboards. By the time he'd shoveled most of it up, he'd filled a fifty-five gallon barrel, and that was just what hadn't run out the hole in the floor. "If you ain't made omelet, you ain't hauled eggs."

Salvaged, broken ones go into dog food, not wholesaled to Denny's or McDonalds. But the scrawny hens that get worn out from laying end up as McNuggets.

Sometimes we shared the CB moment separated by a mile marker or two. But normally, we'd be engrossed with an audio book, the CB mic on its hook, so our impression of other drivers came from those we'd sit with at a table in a Schneider OC or meet at a factory loading dock somewhere. Face to face with other Schneider drivers was always positive. There was camaraderie among us in the Schneider Operating Centers and on the road. We always waved through the windshield at orange pumpkins going the other way on the highway, and they waved back. It was a little thing, a comforting gesture. You could, if not careful, make a mistake and find yourself waving at an orange and black Allied moving van. Embarrassing, but it's over in a second.

Generally there exists a cooperative attitude among most truck drivers regardless of company affiliation. They are always eager to give helpful answers to questions broadcast on the CB. Last minute clarifications for local directions were commonplace.

Even as ex-white-collar workers accustomed to office jobs, we had little difficulty fitting into a mainly blue-collar labor force inside truck stops and terminals. Face to face, drivers are an extremely polite group. We normally wore some kind of clothing that identified us with Schneider. We didn't mind getting our hands dirty or unloading a trailer. It was good exercise and Schneider added a little supplemental pay for unloading. Both of us shared equally in the menial parts of this job, scrubbing a night's worth of bugs off our windshield and sweeping out a dirty trailer. If we had to put on chains, both of us climbed into our overalls, put on leather work gloves, and manhandled the equipment. And we had to do that a number of times.

But this community had a distinctly anti-social, independent, nasty nature as well. David's CB voice didn't sound exactly like one of the guys, so his pleas for information, even for a simple radio check, often went unanswered. In a pinch, I'd make the call and get a quick response. A woman's voice on the CB is wolf bait. But David had to beg me to do it, because I hated talking on the CB. It's a sexist world, demeaning, and given the choice, I switched the CB off when I drove. Unless bad road conditions required that I listen to drivers share advice about slippery spots and wrecks, no CB ever.

I believed David when he said he'd never heard anything as bad, not in the Air Force, fraternity, or locker room. Hiding behind anonymity, CB talk was obscene, senseless, crass, and supremely racist.

Nor was commercial driving the road to respect. The worst part of being a truck driver is like the worst part of being Rodney Dangerfield: "No respect." We got no respect from many in the driving public who generalize and see all trucks as road hazards, nor from crude male drivers who insult women behind the anonymity of a CB radio, nor from the customer because, of course, they are the customer, nor from the Department of Transportation where the atmosphere is adversarial, and not surprisingly, from law enforcement, where you are the enemy. The exception is the enormous respect truckers receive at truck stops where, at each visit, they usually spend $200 or more for fuel. So if it's respect you're looking for, this job isn't your first choice. This is David's best story:

Subject: "Let's You and Him Fight"

I wasn't sure if I should to get fuel at East Sinclair, Wyoming, or go on to Fort Bridger, so I pulled off on the off-ramp at East Sinclair, parked as far to the right as possible to do some quick fuel calculations. Two minutes later a shiny tanker squeezed by and the guy said on the CB radio, "Schneider, that's no place to park."

I fumbled for the microphone to reply that he was right, but I just needed a second to decide if I really wanted to get off on that cross road or not, when suddenly, before I could actually transmit anything this voice came back, "Fuck you asshole Nigger!" in an indignant, asking-for-trouble kind of voice.

Well, no self-respecting driver is going to take that. The shiny tanker sort of finished his right turn onto the crossroad and came back, "Who the hell you think you're talking to?" And the mystery voice from the truck stop wades right in with, "Talking to you at the exit, dumb fuck."

So far I hadn't said a word, but someone was doing his best to do my talking for me. I quickly weighed options as the shiny tanker came to a halt on the shoulder of the crossroad muttering, "We'll see who's a dumb fuck." I never got beyond option one which was to shoot across the crossroad in second gear, down the on-ramp and on up the interstate to Fort Bridger.

We all came out winners. The joker had his joke, the tanker proved he was a man, I stretched my fuel another one hundred fifty miles before refueling and I didn't have to learn to square dance with a guy.

Another bad thing about truck driving is the learning curve. I hate long ones, and I particularly hate feeling perpetually incompetent. Backing up to a loading dock was intimidating, so intimidating that I never once did it right. Ever since road training with Justin, who failed fourteen out of fifteen times trying to talk me through it, David parked the truck at docks. If he was asleep, he woke up. He was the reason we were able to keep driving because if docking depended on me, we'd have washed out on the first load. "Men's work," David used to say and showed uncharacteristic patience. This kind of parking experience in New Haven early in our career honed his skills:

Subject: Parking practice

A load in downtown New Haven gave me a chance to develop close maneuvering skills with the 53' trailer. The loading dock was under a six-lane interstate highway flyway in a rundown part of town. I had to make a U-turn and back up along the wall of the building through an obstacle course which included a dozen concrete columns supporting the flyway, cars parked between each of them. It took ten or twelve forwards and reverses to wiggle in there with Shelley on the walkie-talkie warning me just millimeters before I touched a car, fire hydrant, concrete column, brick wall, or the trailer jack-knifed into the fiberglass cab fairings. When it was all done, the guys on the dock said they'd never seen a 53-footer in there before.

There was nobody to bail us out, so we gave it our best shot, bungled through as a team and next time were better prepared and less intimidated. There are many firsts on that learning curve that once you've done them contribute to self-confidence. Sometimes they're little things. For instance, it's not always apparent the first time you get to a destination what you're supposed to do next especially if there's no guard house. Shipping and receiving offices aren't necessarily marked, and there were many times one of us walked the perimeter of a run-down warehouse at midnight looking for a door, a human, anything resembling a consignee until finally we banged on a door that opened. That was usually my job while David watched in the truck for muggers.

Sometimes we'd find ourselves pulling up to our destination to find that the loading dock was occupied and the only place to wait was straddling the centerline of a city street. The first time you do that, you think something must be wrong with this picture. Only reassurance from the front office that that's the way it's been done for years calms the nerves.

The first time we got lost was memorable. We were in a parking lot. Here's David's email about that experience:

Subject: Lost

Tuesday night in Madison, Maine, at Madison Newspaper, Inc. we picked up our 44,000 pound load of newsprint in a back alley behind the paper mill and headed out into the snow and freezing drizzle. Two inches of new snow showed clearly where the previous truck had turned down a steep little drive to circle around behind some pulp tanks and get to the exit gate. On the other hand, there were some older tracks, many more actually, that went straight ahead into the darkness. Maybe that was the way out.

We chose the right hand turn, sort of an acrobatic tight and steep turn on fresh snow to a driveway along the river that came to a total dead-end. Now what? The tracks we'd followed seemed to reverse and back right out the way they came in. How had he done that? No room to turn around. Just then the local driveway plowing guy came by in his pick-up and plowed the track down to the base course of packed snow and loose gravel. Meanwhile Shelley and I got out the chains and put one on each of the four outer drive tires.

The problem we faced was what's called a "blind side back" up the slope into the driveway we had come out of. With the trailer curving toward the passenger side my only mirror was an eight-inch diameter fish eye spherical mirror on the passenger side and at night, it is useless to me. Maybe some other drivers can see something in such a mirror but not me, not at night. With Shelley on the remote CB guiding me either tighter or looser to the inside of the curve, I gave it four attempts, each one a little faster and more reckless than the previous. But each ended with spinning drive tires and zero velocity halfway up the slope.

Then the Mainer with the snowplow pick-up had a suggestion: do a normal "driver's side back" up the hill. That way the turn would be more gradual, the slope a little less steep, and I could see what I was doing. Of course, we would be facing the wrong way at the top of the hill, but at that time of night there were no more trucks waiting to be loaded, so we could go out the "in" gate, no problem. That worked, and we didn't have to wait at the bottom of the hill for a wrecker.

During the early months of learning, we captured on endless videotape every inaugural crossing of America's biggest bridges. It is probably the most boring six hours of video in existence, but riveting to us. Here is our email about the first time we used the second level westbound across the George Washington Bridge, a New York landmark, and memorable in more ways than architectural:

Subject: David does The Big Apple

The approach to the George Washington Bridge westbound from the Manhattan side is a series of climbing spiral ramps. The final spiral is a 360 degree left-hand corkscrew with merging traffic near the top. I found myself paired up with another long semi. I ended up in the left (inside) lane and the other truck was in the right (outside) lane. It quickly dawned on me there wasn't room for both of us, well just barely.

Picture how a semi's trailer wheels cut the corner during a tight turn. My trailer wheels were following a path about two feet left of the track followed by the steering wheels. I was steering along the right side of my lane in order to keep from jumping the left hand curb with my trailer wheels; and the other guy had his steering wheels kissing the extreme right curb of his lane to keep his trailer from scraping the right side of my truck. The first clue as to the seriousness of the situation was when Shelley pointed out that his trailer was about to adjust the rear view mirrors two feet from her face. At this point he was slightly ahead as we both tailgated as close as possible to the traffic creeping up this steep, tight, counter-clockwise spiral.

My attention was dancing from the left mirror that showed my trailer tires scraping the left curb to the right mirror that I was trying to keep three inches from his trailer. On the CB radio I asked for a little daylight, but no response, and his eyes stayed glued straight ahead. We continued nip and tuck with him a car length ahead for a quarter of the circle when it occurred to me that if I had to stop because of a slow car ahead, he'd have to stop also or drag his trailer through my right side mirrors and maybe Shelley's door too, because the part of his trailer three inches away was near the front of his trailer. The back of his trailer was way over the centerline. I just had to win the race. I couldn't speed up because of the car in front; I couldn't stop for fear of total wipeout; I couldn't give room to the left without jumping the curb and damaging the trailer tires. So we crabbed along like a pair of parallel skis around a slalom pole.

What I didn't know until the last second was that the two lanes merge into one at the end of the corkscrew. Just as I realized that, Shelley yelled, "He's merging!" and I yanked the wheel to the left, sacrificed the trailer tires to the mercy of the curb, and hit the brakes. The big New York truck slid past with a triumphant glance in his mirrors, and the whole lower level westbound halted while the Schneider got his truck back on the roadway and underway again. No harm done. Just another example of why many of the truck driver recruiting ads in magazines proudly proclaim, "No East Coast Deliveries" along with the normal stuff like free health insurance, new trucks, high pay.

If you're clever, you can roll up a number of firsts into one: first time you do something grossly illegal, unsafe, scenic, daring, and dumb. Here's how we remember the first time we made the mistake of choosing State Highway 14 on the Washington side of the Columbia River gorge:

Subject: Friday the Thirteenth

How was your Friday the 13th?

Mine started lucky enough at 04:00 in a soft thirty-three degree rain. We decided to try a new Skinny Road – Washington Highway 14 along the north bluff of the Columbia River Gorge. We'd been up and down the south side on the interstate several times but always longed to see the other side. We could see the highway cut into the bluffs over there. It was a designated truck route on our atlas and had the "green dotted" designation used for scenic two-lane roads. Friday we had six hours available to drive 250 miles to our appointment with Chrysler in Beaverton, so it was a good opportunity to take the slow road.

We were not disappointed by Washington Highway 14. New pavement, gentle hills and curves, commanding view of the river, cliffs, barges and tugs, dams, locks, and dry grasslands gradually replaced by rain forest as we approached the Pacific.

It was the rainy season. From rock cuts and natural cliffs, hundreds of waterfalls large and small leaped out at us and fell short except for one which came from such height that the breeze carried it over the pavement as it fell.

It is the tunnels, however, we will remember. This is an old historic highway. The seven tunnels were dug long before current size limits were standardized. We are 102" wide and 13'-6" high — dimensions drilled into us from our first day at truck driving school eight months ago. These old tunnels were lined with concrete at the entrances only, the rest bare rock just as it was chiseled out by old world masons. The profile is arched at the top and the sides are straight and vertical. Lovely to look at.

Before you go wandering around the country with a 102" by 13'-6" trailer you are well-advised to check the route to make sure of several things:

1. Is the highway designated as a route for full-size trucks?

2. Does the state allow full-size trucks on its undesignated state highways?

3. Are there any sections of your route that have low clearance bridges?

4. Are there any sections of your route that are restricted "no truck" routes?

Shelley says she checked our Rand McNally Motor Carrier's Road Atlas to see if Washington-14 had any problems like that, but she must have looked at the Oregon section, or she was looking for US-14 instead of WA-14. I never checked the fine print; I just noted that WA-14 is color-coded as a designated truck route. Anyway, we missed a few items of interest for any trucker planning to cruise the north shore of the Columbia:

1. Under restricted routes, "WA-14 from Mt. Pleasant east to unnumbered route." On close inspection a tiny 1/4" section of the road is *not* color coded as a truck route.

2. In the low clearance section, "Two tunnels approx. 1 mi. East of Lyle, minimum height 9'-0". Five tunnels between Cook and Underwood, minimum height 12'-9".

See where this is leading? Halfway on our one hundred eighty mile Columbia River cruise, we enjoyed the little town of Lyle and, just west, two cute old tunnels. Shelley was charmed by the state's installation of self-activated warning lights so bikers could initiate five minutes of flashing lights before entering a tunnel, and drivers would thereby use extra caution. I was impressed by the raw rock walls and gradually moved toward the centerline just to make sure no sharp rock unzipped the side of the trailer. We saw no low clearance sign.

Then fifty miles later we got the wake-up call about the tunnels on this scenic road. Big yellow warning sign, "Low tunnels. 13'-0". I pulled onto the narrow shoulder with a foot of trailer still in the traffic lane, the gaping mouth of the tunnel twenty feet away.

What to do? We got out the atlas and discovered the warning notations. We realized we'd already been through the lowest of the seven tunnels – 9'0". So, why hadn't we hit something? The minimum height is measured at the edge of the pavement. Out there the arched ceilings are much lower than in the center of the arch. The center was over sixteen feet. By dumb luck I must have been far enough over the centerline to miss any features lower than 13'-6" and breezed though happy as a drooling idiot. I've seen trailers after contact with a bridge at highway speed. Not pretty, but this was Lucky Friday the Thirteenth.

So, would we be lucky in the rest of the tunnels? With any on-coming traffic, we'd be creamed. There are four bridges on the route to cross over to the I-84 side. To turn around was impossible. To back up five miles to the last town at three miles per hour would require a police escort. We had just reported to Schneider and Chrysler that we were on schedule for 10:00 delivery.

Denial: "This isn't happening."

Anger: "Those bastards, why didn't anyone put a warning sign at the beginning of the road."

Grief: "We're screwed."

Acceptance: "There's gotta be a way through these things."

A passing log trucker told us on the CB radio that we could go through, just stay away from the sides. Easy for him to say. His load of logs was high in the middle, low on the sides. I got off the truck, trotted up to the chiseled hole in the rock to take a look. As highway tunnels go, it had a pretty sharp right-hand curve built into it. The trailer would trail a couple of feet out to the right side. Even if I drove down the centerline, would the trailer corners touch?

Well, as you may have guessed, we are not still sitting there on the side of WA-14. Shelley jumped out and punched the bicycler's warning button. Strobe lights started flashing. We pulled out and crept down the centerline while traffic piled up behind, but none came at us from the opposite direction. Shelley craned her head out the window and saw at least eighteen inches of daylight around the trailing top corner of our trailer. No sweat. The next four tunnels were straight, not curved and we didn't slow down much for them, just straddled the centerline. One had a 4-wheeler coming in the opposite direction so I gave him all but two feet of his lane. Didn't hear or feel anything out of the ordinary so guess he made it okay. And so did we.

Pulling our first hazmat load is a first we'll never forget. Ours was in Mountain Pass, California, at a rare earth mine with radioactive by-products on site. All visitors had to go through a little training procedure at the gate before they were allowed on the lot. We were issued respirators and taught how to use them in an emergency, what the warning signal sounded like, what all-clear sounded like, and where the safety zones were for the time in-between. When we finished, we were given certificates which would allow us in again without re-training, but that was our first and last load of cerium. Reading and understanding hazmat paperwork, re-familiarizing yourself with regulations, understanding what placards are required is a complicated subject and is far more real than reading about it in a manual. It's one of those things you need to do right, but the next time with our Chrysler load of airbag explosives, it seemed easy.

Schneider's training program — probably as good as it gets — eased our entry into the profession and softened the learning curve. During the first two years, our enthusiasm for the job seldom lagged and Schneider was as good a boss as one could expect. They weren't Hewlett-Packard, but within the trucking industry the company was professional, cutting edge, and they accommodated our style of driving with flexible schedules and a wide variety of destinations. We found what we'd been looking for in this job: good pay, adventure, relaxed work days. Compared to others we'd both had, it ranked among the best.

By year three, we were approaching the end of the honeymoon. Whether it was the inevitable evolution of truck driving in particular or whether any job, anywhere would eventually lose its blush is hard to know. For whatever reason, the scales tipped toward it feeling more like work than adventure. Even sailing in the West Indies after eight months lost its tinsel.

Twenty-five years ago we were living aboard a comfortable yacht in tropical waters, among lush islands, and with more income than expenses. Yet, we decided we'd had enough and we returned to a settled life in Wisconsin. If paradise couldn't hold our interest forever, there's not much hope that trucking would either.

If you think about it, trying to squeeze in an alternate career before retirement is a tall order. What other good-paying job was as available as truck driving? What other job allowed the two of us to work together? What other job had free training? What other job wasn't boring? What other job came packed with surprises every day — new destinations, new states, roads and towns, new adventure?

Team driving fits into a variety of lifestyles. Young couples with no children or retirees with grown children would enjoy the life we enjoyed. Couples who need to cut expenses while saving money for a down payment on a house or some other major purchase are good candidates for trucking. Expenses on the road are relatively few and the IRS allows a generous per diem meal deduction. Cutting expenses at home is easy, too: cancel cable or satellite TV; reduce living quarters to the basics because most of the time you're in a truck away from home anyway; pocket your wardrobe allowance; save on booze; sell the second car and reduce insurance on your beater; let Schneider pay the doctor's bills; and in David's case, grow a ponytail.

So if it was so wonderful, why did we stop? Easy answer: we'd saved enough money to retire. Coupled with social security when David became eligible and the considerable nest egg we'd saved during our three years of driving, plus a booming stock market, we didn't need much more money — a nice position to be in. David was eager to use his woodworking workshop to make the furniture he'd been designing in his head while truck driving. And although we could stow an enormous amount of baggage in that orange truck, the table saw was another matter.

Would we do it again? In an r.p.m. We're keeping our CDL's current.

About the authors

Shelley Hamel lives with her husband, David, on 110 acres of sand prairie and bog near Westfield, Wisconsin. After retiring from three years of truck driving, they spend spring, summer, and fall restoring habitat for a federally-endangered butterfly called the *Karner Blue* that lives amid the native lupine plants on their prairie.

In winters, they often head out, once to the Aleutian Islands to spend eight months caretaking an off-the-grid homestead in the Isanotski Strait and most recently to San Miguel de Allende, Mexico, to inn-sit a Bed and Breakfast for a winter.

Also by Shelley Hamel

WINTER FISH – 12 Hours in a Van

Made in the USA
Columbia, SC
30 December 2018